Smart RV Travel Guide for the Lower 48 States

List of RV & National Parks, the Cost, the Amenities, What to See and Do in Each State

By

Ron Samson

TABLE OF CONTENTS

INTRODUCTION

Nothing is more enjoyable than traveling the country in an RV. You can go pretty much anywhere, and with a little planning, you can do it on a budget, so you have money to spend on visiting attractions. First, we need to discuss where you are going to stay and how you can do it for free or cheap before we start looking at destinations you can visit.

First, you want to understand the difference between RV camping and parking. Simply put:

RV Camping = Multiple days stay.

RV Parking = A place to spend the night.

You can find a variety of free RV parking on both public and private lands if you simply need a place to stay for the night. Free RV camping, on the other hand, is often done on public lands. If you simply need to park somewhere overnight for free then consider the following options:

> Truck stops
> Walmart
> Nightclubs
> Fraternal organizations
> Cemeteries
> Fairgrounds
> Parks
> Churches
> Hotels

- ➢ Truck terminals
- ➢ RV dealers
- ➢ Cracker Barrel
- ➢ Movie theaters
- ➢ Highway rest areas
- ➢ Big box retailers
- ➢ Picnic areas

Overnight parking is often influenced by city and county ordinances. It's always good to check with the local police or a store manager first.

If you need to stay more than a night you have three main options.

The first option is full hookup camping. While this can often be the most expensive, you can find deals. Full hookups typically come with electric, water and sewer hookups; but some will even have other amenities such as cable or telephone. Most campsites that offer full hookups also give you the option of a partial hookup for a discounted rate.

You can also get a discount on full hookup camping by buying a membership in a discount camping club. Often memberships cost under $100 and can give you discounts up to 50% off.

A second option is staying at casinos. Many casinos have separate parking lots just for RVs and allow free overnight stays or even multi-day stays. A few casinos even come with amenities. Be sure to call ahead or check in with casino security when you arrive to see what is allowed.

The last option is called boondocking or dry camping. This is often done in natural areas without any amenities. This is often the cheapest form of RV camping since there are no amenities involved. Boondocking is typically done on public lands such as Bureau of Land Management lands.

Boondocking as a general rule is allowed anywhere on federal public lands within a specific distance of an established road unless there are restrictions. The idea is to use a previous campsite area or use an area in a way your vehicle won't damage it. You will need to check locally for requirements in your area. The most common restriction is that you can't camp within 300 feet of a water source.

When it comes to BLM and USFS lands, the general rule is that you can stay 14 continuous days for free then you must travel 25 miles away. The BLM Long Term Visitor Areas will allow stays of several months for a small fee.

The real work begins when you try to find the best boondocking locations. Where you can boondock often depends on the size and type RV you have. Pop up, and truck campers can often get to more remote sites. When it comes to looking for boondocking sites you need four main things:

1. Maps and navigational information.
2. Contact information for Public Lands Administrators.
3. A base campground.
4. A sense of exploration.

Once you know, the general area you want to boondock in you will need to get some general information. Having official travel maps can be helpful, but topographical maps are best. After you have a location in mind, you will need to contact the local Public Lands Administrators to ask about dispersed camping in the area. Always make sure to keep in mind potential weather changes and how it can affect road conditions to and from the location you want to camp.

Now that you are prepared to find a spot to stay. Let's see what there is to see in all the states.

(Credit – www.EnchantedLearning.com)

Alabama is a wonderful state full of southern hospitality. You can take a trip in forested hills to the north or enjoy sandy shores in the south. There is also plenty of history to enjoy while in Alabama. No matter what your interest there is something to enjoy in Alabama.

The southern seaboard of Alabama takes up 60 miles along the Gulf of Mexico. The shores of Alabama aren't as famous as other states, but they are just as beautiful as the Emerald Coast of Florida. Along the seaside towns of Gulf Shores, you'll find plenty of beach activities and wonderful dining options.

Once you leave the coast, you may want to enjoy the oldest and most beautiful city in Alabama. Mobile is the second largest city of Alabama and the oldest with some of the most beautiful historic plantation homes you will ever see on this coast. Let's also not forget that Mobile is the original birth place of famous Mardi Gras festival. Mobile Mardi Gras was founded by the Roman Catholics from France in 1702, was home to the first **Mystic** society, or "krewe," which held America's first Mardi Gras celebration in 1704 — 14 years before **New Orleans** was even founded. Even though New Orleans is known for their Mardi Gras, Mobile still offers the best family oriented and the most original Mardi Gras parades every year around February.

If you want to hang out in the city, head to Birmingham; the largest city in Alabama. In this town, there are plenty of entertainment options and historical museums. No matter what your interest there will be museums to enjoy. Plus to the east, there is Talladega, home to NASCAR competition. In the northern part of the state, there is the city of Huntsville, which offers plenty of options for space enthusiasts.

Alabama offers warm weather throughout most of the year, making it a great travel destination. If you plan on taking an RV trip through this state consider the following recommended trip and what you can see along the way.

SUGGESTED ALABAMA RV TRIP

If you are only going to make one RV trip in Alabama, you want to visit the Gulf Coast. Start in Gulf Shores and end in Mobile. This trip is 51 miles and takes about 1 hour and 20 minutes to drive, offering you plenty of time to stay and enjoy the local activities along the way. This trip offers beautiful beaches, quaint towns and plenty of dining experiences.

Start off in the beautiful beachside community of Gulf Shores, which is one of the top 10 destinations in Alabama. Here you can enjoy water activities such as swimming, kayaking, and stand-up paddle boarding. You can choose to go bird watching along the Gulf Coast Birding Trail or go into town for the Alabama Gulf Coast Zoo, the Gulf Shores Museum and the Waterville USA water park.

A 32-mile drive of about 48 minutes brings you to the town of Fairhope. This town is known for a mix of natural beauty and historic sites. In the Fairhope French Quarter, you'll find the largest crape myrtle tree in the American South. You can also experience a number of beautiful culinary experiences while here.

Lastly, a short 19-mile drive of about 32 minutes brings you to the end of the trip in Mobile. This town has plenty of historical attractions, parks, and museums. It is home to another top 10 destinations with the USS Alabama Battleship Memorial Park.

SUGGESTED RV PARK

In Mobile, you will find the All About Relaxing RV Park. Rates are about $38 to $52. Pets are welcome at the 41 sites available in this park. The park offers the following amenities:

- ★ Restroom and Showers
- ★ Laundry
- ★ Self-Service RV Wash
- ★ Internet
- ★ Swimming Pool
- ★ Horseshoes
- ★ Recreation Hall
- ★ Pavilion

No matter where you plan to go in Alabama be sure to check out the following state parks for good RV camping.

RV CAMPING AT ALABAMA STATE PARKS

AMENITIES

- Typical cost: $13-$60 with some parks offering weekly deals.
- Water: Always
- Electric: Always
- Sewer: Usually with 19 out of 21 parks with RV spots.
- Laundry: Often
- There is no maximum stay limit.

STATE PARKS WITH FULL RV HOOKUPS

- ❑ Buck's Pocket (4 full hookups out of 36)
- ❑ DeSoto (94 full hookups)
- ❑ Joe Wheeler (110 full hookups out of 116)
- ❑ Lake Guntersville (318 sites with some being full hookups)
- ❑ Monte Sano (17 full hookups out of 78)
- ❑ Cheaha Resort (72 full hookups)
- ❑ Lake Lurleen (35 full hookup sites out of 91)
- ❑ Oak Mountain (85 full hookup sites out of 60)
- ❑ Wind Creek (268 full hookup sites out of 586)
- ❑ Blue Springs (7 full hookup sites out of 50)
- ❑ Chewacla (36 sites, including satellite TV)
- ❑ Florala (28 full hookup sites)
- ❑ Frank Jackson (32 full hookup sites including WiFi and cable)
- ❑ Deer Court (192 sites, but not all offer full hookups)
- ❑ Paul M. Grist (11 full hookup sites)
- ❑ Roland Cooper (47 full hookup sites and 13 primitive sites)
- ❑ Bladon Springs (10 full hookup sites)
- ❑ Gulf (496 full hookup sites)
- ❑ Meaher (61 full hookup sites)

The following sites only have water and electric hookups

- ❑ Chickasaw (3 sites with water and electric only)
- ❑ Rickwood Caverns (9 sites that can accommodate RVs)

(Credit – www.theodora.com/maps)

Throughout Arizona, you will see a beautiful rugged landscape that helped shape Native American and Old West history. Arizona features everything from natural beauty, old west history to urban cultural areas; no matter what your travel preferences you'll find something to do in Arizona.

If you want to enjoy nature, you won't get any better than Sedona. In this area, you will find a number of ways to enjoy epic nature views including horseback riding, rock climbing, and off-roading. However, Sedona also offers a downtown urban area with plenty of cultural sites to see.

If a city trip is more your speed, then there are plenty of wonderful cities with metropolitan environments to visit in Arizona. Phoenix is the capital of Arizona and its largest city with beautiful weather all year. In Phoenix, there are plenty of cultural options to visit including the Musical Instrument Museum, the Heard Museum, and the Desert Botanical Garden. The second largest city in the state is Tucson which offers places such as the Arizona-Sonora Desert Museum and the Tucson Botanical Gardens. Then there is Flagstaff, where you can find cooler temperatures and year-round outdoor activities; including snow in the winter.

Perhaps the most distinctive natural landmark in Arizona is the Grand Canyon. This marvel of nature is over a mile deep in some places and is visited by some six million a year. You can enjoy the views from the top or take adventurous trips into the depths of the canyon. Often the South Rim of the canyon is busy with tourist stops while the North Rim features a more quiet, nature experience.

Another famous stop in Arizona is the Four Corners region. Here the borders of Utah, Arizona, Colorado and New Mexico meet at a monument. Nearby you'll also find the beautiful formations of Monument Valley.

If you want to enjoy the water while in Arizona then you need to visit Yuma and the nearby Lake Havasu. Yuma offers the most hours of sunlight per year and offers great access to the Colorado River. To the north, Lake Havasu offers plenty of options for boaters, anglers and those who just want a lazy day on the water. Lake Havasu is also home to the London Bridge and an English Village, for those who want to take a trip out of the country without actually getting on a plane.

SUGGESTED ARIZONA RV TRIPS

There are two wonderful RV trips to take in Arizona, depending on the sites you want to see. For a more tourist-oriented trip, you should do the Arizona North tour of the Grand Canyon and surrounding area. For a quieter trip away from it all take the Arizona South tour through some nice small towns.

The Arizona North trip is 400.8 miles and takes about 7 hours to drive. It starts in Phoenix and circles around to Wickenburg and back to Phoenix. Phoenix is the capital city of Arizona and the perfect spot to start your journey. While most view Phoenix as a simple stopover, you may want to take some time enjoying the outdoors here by hiking Camelback Mountain or learning about the local flora by visiting the Desert Botanical Garden. While in Phoenix there are four wonderful activities you can do for free.

First, you can visit the Phoenix Art Museum on one of their many free days. Admission is free Wednesday evenings from 3-9pm; the first Friday from 6-10pm and the second Sunday from 12-5pm. If you visit on a Sunday, you'll even be able to take part in art-making with local artists, scavenger hunts, live performances and free guided tours.

Second, on the first Friday of every month from 6-10pm you can take part in Art Walk. This is one of the largest self-guided art walks in the United States. There is also a free trolley. On this day you can also get into the Heard Museum of Native Cultures and Art for free as well.

Third, is to take a hike up Camelback Mountain. At an elevation of 2,704 feet it is a strenuous hike, but short. The mountain features two trails, both with free parking or you can take a free trolley to the trailhead.

Lastly, it is always free to visit the Arizona Capitol Museum. Here you can view artifacts from the USS Arizona that was sunk during Pearl Harbor as well as interactive exhibits about the states' role in World War II. Each day there are also guided tours available for free.

Next, take about a 116 mile or about 2-hour drive to the town of Sedona. This town is nestled among the red rocks that make the area famous. On your drive to this town be sure to stop by the Montezuma Castle National Monument where you can hike up Cathedral Rock for stunning views of the surrounding area. On your way to the next destination, you'll come to a suggested RV park.

SUGGESTED RV PARK IN CAMP VERDE

In the small town of Camp Verde, you'll find the Distant Drums RV Resort, it is actually just south of Sedona. It is open all year and has an average cost of $38 to $46. Pets are welcome with an enclosed dog run available. There is a total of 156 sites at this park, and it offers the following amenities:

★ Internet

- ★ Restroom and Showers
- ★ Laundry
- ★ RV Supplies
- ★ Metered LP Gas
- ★ Ice
- ★ Cable
- ★ Heated Pool
- ★ Hot Tub
- ★ Horseshoes
- ★ Recreation Hall
- ★ Game Room
- ★ Pavilion
- ★ Exercise Room
- ★ Nature Trails

Continue your trip about 58 miles or 54 minutes into Flagstaff. Here the temperature starts to drop because of the altitude. Flagstaff is a laid-back area to stage your trip to the Grand Canyon. Here you can visit the beautiful Arboretum at Flagstaff or the historic Lowell Observatory where Pluto was first discovered. If visiting in the summer, you can enjoy Movies on the Square each Friday at 3 pm for free. Also between June and August, you can enjoy Concerts in the Park on Wednesdays starting at 5:30 pm for free.

SUGGESTED RV PARK IN WILLIAMS

In the small town of Williams, you'll find another recommended RV park, the Grand Canyon Railway RV Park. This park is open all year and averages $43 to $48. This park welcomes pets and has a total of 124 RV sites. The park features the following amenities:

- ★ Internet
- ★ Restroom and Showers
- ★ Laundry
- ★ ATM
- ★ RV Supplies
- ★ Ice
- ★ Groceries
- ★ Restaurant
- ★ Cable
- ★ Heated Pool
- ★ Hot Tub
- ★ Horseshoes
- ★ Game Room
- ★ Playground
- ★ Pavilion
- ★ Exercise Room

Next, take the short drive of thirteen miles or sixteen minutes to Kaibab National Forest. At this park, you can hike a portion of the 800 mile Arizona Trail.

From here it is an 88 mile, about an hour and a half drive to the town of Prescott. This historic city was once the territorial capital of Arizona in 1864. As you walk through the town you can visit Whiskey Row which is dominated by Old West saloons.

The last leg of your trip is about 58 miles or almost an hour and a half to Wickenburg. This historic city practically oozes Wild West history. Here you can visit the Desert Caballeros Western Museum and the Vulture City ghost town with the historic Vulture Mine. You can also do a lot of hiking in the Hassayampa River Preserve. The drive back to Phoenix to complete the trip is about 66 miles or just over an hour.

The second RV trip in Arizona takes you through some of the smaller towns in the southern part of the state. The total trip is about 254 miles and takes about 4 hours. It starts in Yuma and ends in Tucson.

This trip starts in the southwestern corner of the state in Yuma. This area is popular with people seeking outdoor recreation. Since it is close to the Colorado River, you also have the option of kayaking, canoeing, and swimming. The town itself is best known for the Yuma Territorial Prison State Historic Park. This area is also home to some excellent RV parks.

SUGGESTED RV PARKS IN YUMA

In Yuma, there is the Blue Sky Ranch RV Resort. This pet-friendly resort has a total of 200 spaces and costs about $37 to $45 all year. It comes with the following amenities:

- ★ Internet
- ★ Restroom and Showers
- ★ Laundry
- ★ Heated Pool
- ★ Hot Tub
- ★ Recreation Hall

- ★ Outdoor Games
- ★ Pavilion
- ★ Shuffleboard
- ★ Pickle Ball
- ★ Putting Green

Another option is the Fortuna de Oro RV Resort in the foothills of Yuma. This park costs $42 to $52 all year and features an impressive nearly 1300 spaces at this pet-friendly resort. It also features the following amenities:

- ★ Internet
- ★ Restroom and Showers
- ★ Laundry
- ★ ATM
- ★ Ice
- ★ Worship Services
- ★ Restaurant
- ★ Heated Pool
- ★ Hot Tub
- ★ Horseshoes
- ★ Recreation Hall
- ★ Game Room
- ★ Outdoor Games
- ★ Golf Course
- ★ Driving Range
- ★ Pavilion
- ★ Tennis Court
- ★ Shuffleboard
- ★ Exercise Room

★ Frisbee Golf

★ Pickle Ball

★ Putting Green

A third option is the Sundance RV Resort. This park is open all year long at a rate of $37. The park is pet-friendly with 457 sites. The park comes with the following amenities:

★ Restroom and Showers

★ Laundry

★ Ice

★ Worship Services

★ Cable

★ Self-Service RV Wash

★ Heated Pool

★ Hot Tub

★ Horseshoes

★ Recreation Hall

★ Game Room

★ Shuffleboard

★ Exercise Room

★ Putting Green

★ Pickle Ball

Lastly, there is the Villa Alameda RV Resort. This park is open all year at $35. This pet-friendly resort has 302 spaces. The park has the following amenities:

- ★ Limited Internet
- ★ Restroom and Showers
- ★ Laundry
- ★ Ice
- ★ Worship Services
- ★ Cable
- ★ Self-Service RV Wash
- ★ Heated Pool
- ★ Hot Tub
- ★ Horseshoes
- ★ Recreation Hall
- ★ Game Room
- ★ Outdoor Games
- ★ Shuffleboard

After leaving Yuma, it is a 116 mile, almost two-hour drive to the little town of Gila Bend. This town is close to the ancient Hohokam people and their enigmatic Painted Rock Petroglyph Site. East of town you can also visit the Sonoran Desert National Monument. For the hiker, there is also the Juan Bautista de Anza National Historic Trail that takes you along the path of the 1775 Spanish expedition from Nogales, Arizona to San Francisco.

The next leg of the trip takes you about an hour or 65 miles to get to the town of Casa Grande. Here you are placed near two very neat attractions: Picacho State Park and the Casa Grande Ruins National Monument.

The last leg of the trip takes you about an hour and 73 miles to get to Tucson. Tucson has often been an alternative to Phoenix. It serves as an excellent base to explore the natural beauty of the surrounding area. Hiking in the nearby Saguaro National Park is a great choice, or you can visit the Kitt Peak National Observatory to learn about space. To learn about the local area, visit the Arizona-Sonora Desert Museum. In addition, there are three wonderful activities in the town that you can enjoy for free.

First is the San Xavier Mission that was established in 1732. Here you can learn about Spanish colonial architecture, art, and history. You can also visit the Southern Arizona Transportation Museum for free to learn about the history of transportation in Southern Arizona. Lastly, the second Saturday of each month features free live entertainment in downtown Tucson.

SUGGESTED RV PARK IN TUCSON

At the end of your trip, you can stay awhile at this resort to enjoy all Tucson has to offer. The Far Horizons RV Resort is open year-round at a rate of $35 to $55. This pet-friendly resort has 514 total spaces and offers the following amenities:

- ★ Internet
- ★ Restroom and Showers
- ★ Laundry
- ★ Ice
- ★ Cable
- ★ Guest Services
- ★ Self-Service RV Wash

- ★ Heated Pool
- ★ Hot Tub
- ★ Horseshoes
- ★ Recreation Hall
- ★ Game Room
- ★ Outdoor Games
- ★ Sauna
- ★ Exercise Room
- ★ Nature Trails
- ★ Mini Golf
- ★ Putting Green
- ★ Pickle Ball

RV CAMPING AT ARIZONA STATE PARKS

AMENITIES

- Typical Cost: $15-$50
- Water: Yes
- Electric: Yes
- Sewer: Sometimes at 5 out of 14 parks.
- Laundry: Rarely
- In/Out Rules: You are allowed to stay 14 nights in a 30 night period with some long-term stay parks offering 29 nights in 45 night period.

STATE PARKS WITH FULL RV HOOKUPS

- ❏ Alamo Lake (202 sites)

- ❏ Fool Hollow Lake (123 sites)
- ❏ Lyman Lake (61 sites)
- ❏ Patagonia Lake (100 sites)
- ❏ Picacho Peak (89 sites, closed between May and September)

The following parks only have water and electric hookups

- ❏ Cattail Cover (61 sites)
- ❏ Lake Havasu (47 sites)
- ❏ River Island (37 sites)
- ❏ Dead Horse Ranch (131 sites)
- ❏ Homolovi (52 sites)
- ❏ Catalina State Park (120 sites)
- ❏ Lost Dutchman (134 sites)
- ❏ Kartchner Caverns (62 sites)
- ❏ Roper Lake (58 sites)

ARKANSAS

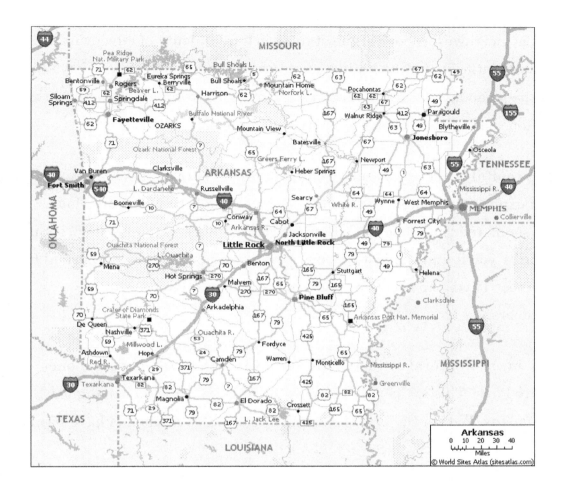

Arkansas is home to a diverse landscape ranging from hills in the north to a lowland delta. In the northwest part of the state, there are plenty of outdoor adventures, the town of Eureka Springs can take you back in history with elegant Victorian homes, Bentonville features a strong cultural arts scene, and Little Rock features a strong urban environment.

No matter what you want to do on your trip, you'll find it in Arkansas. The Ouachita Mountains offers secluded areas of natural with clear lakes and rivers for those who want an outdoor adventure. Following the

Mississippi River for a number of historic Native American cultural sites as well as Civil War battlefields.

In the northwest corner of the state, you'll find plenty of adventure opportunities including hiking, mountain biking, canoeing and kayaking in the legendary Ozark Mountains. There are several state parks in this region that provide plenty of RV travel options.

The capital of the state and its cultural center is Little Rock. Here you can explore the history of the state at places like the Old State House Museum and the Little Rock Central HIgh School National Historic Site. Nearby you'll find the Hot Springs area, which is home to 47 thermal hot springs. This is an excellent place to relax after a long day in the outdoors.

The biggest natural attraction in Arkansas is the Crater of Diamonds State Park. This is the only place in the world where you can dig for diamonds. Within the last 45 years, nearly 30,000 diamonds have been found in the park.

SUGGESTED ARKANSAS RV TRIPS

When traveling through Arkansas in an RV, there is one trip you need to take. The trip a short one of 111 miles and takes about 2 hours but has plenty of things to see and do. It starts out in the city of Little Rock and ends in the small town of Murfreesboro.

In the city of Little Rock, you can visit the state capital and largest city. Take a walk in the River Market District to see a range of stores, events, and entertainment. While visiting this city, there are three free things you can enjoy.

First is the city's visitor information center at the historic Curran Hall and one of only a handful of antebellum homes still remaining in the city. You can also tour the building and gardens.

Second, you can take a walk along the Big Dam Bridge, the world's longest pedestrian, and bicycle bridge. The bridge takes you over, Murray Lock and Dam. This bridge stretches 3,463 feet over the Arkansas River. The bridge also ties together over 15 miles of scenic river trails in the city.

A third thing you can do for free in Little Rock is to visit the Central High School from 1927. This school gained international attention during the Civil Rights Movement and today houses a museum that tells the story of what happened at the school in 1957.

The second portion of your trip will take you about an hour and 54 miles to the town of Hot Springs. This town is located within the Ouachita Mountains and is popular with those seeking a wellness retreat because of the mineral-rich thermal hot springs. Nearby Lake Catherine also gives you plenty of options for boating and fishing, while Lake Hamilton is great for waterskiing.

The last leg of the trip is about an hour drive and 56 miles to Murfreesboro. Perhaps the best-known attraction here is the Crater of Diamonds State Park, where you can actually search for real diamonds. You can also find other gems in the area. Plus there is a water park and hiking trails in the area.

RV CAMPING AT ARKANSAS STATE PARKS

AMENITIES

- Typical Cost: $12-$32
- Water: Yes
- Electric: Yes
- Sewer: Usually (12 out of 20 parks)
- In/Out Rules: No maximum limits.

ARKANSAS STATE PARKS

- ❑ Bull Shoals-White River (34 full hookups & 48 water & electric only)
- ❑ Cane Creek (29 water & electric only)
- ❑ Crater of Diamonds (47 full hookups)
- ❑ Lake Catherine (44 full hookups & 25 water & electric only)
- ❑ Lake Charles (9 full hookups & 59 water & electric only)
- ❑ Lake Chicot (55 full hookups & 67 water & electric only)
- ❑ Lake Dardanelle (30 full hookups & 47 water & electric only)
- ❑ Lake Fort Smith (20 full hookups & 10 water & electric only)
- ❑ Lake Frierson (4 water & electric only & 3 primitive sites)
- ❑ Lake Ouachita (40 full hookups, 25 water & electric only & 24 primitive sites)
- ❑ Lake Poinsett (26 water & electric only)
- ❑ Millwood (2 full hookups & 112 water & electric only)
- ❑ Mississippi River (14 full hookups & 17 primitive sites)
- ❑ Morro Bay (20 water & electric only)

- Mount Magazine (18 full hookups)
- Mount Nebo (24 water & electric only)
- Petit Jean (35 full hookups & 90 water & electric only)
- Queen Wilhelmina (35 water & electric only)
- Village Creek (96 water & electric only)
- White Oak Lake (41 water & electric only)

CALIFORNIA

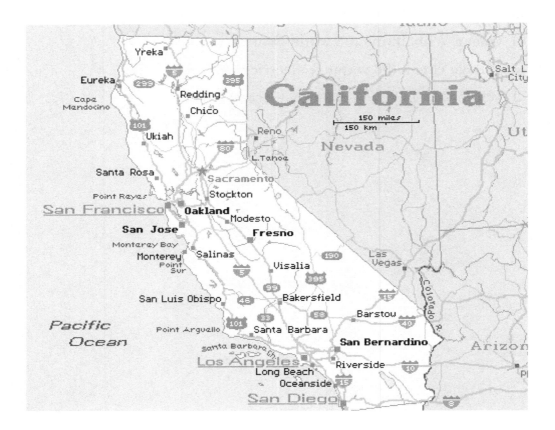

If any state truly has it all, it's California. This state features a broad range of geological and cultural influences. From redwood forests to the agricultural Central Valley to the snow-filled Sierra Nevada to the huge metropolitan cities to the unique beach towns; there is plenty to see and do in California. The biggest draw for many in California is the great outdoors. In the span of a day, you can take a hike through forests, deserts, and beaches. Whether you like to hike, bike, surf or dive you will find an outdoor adventure. Even those who want a more urban adventure, will find plenty of activities and sites to see in California.

California is full of well-known cities: Los Angeles, Malibu, Santa Monica, and San Francisco. Santa Monica features a strong cultural and art scene as well as outdoor activities and events for all types of people. San Francisco is easily one of the top cities in America and features a number of iconic sites and budget friendly travel options.

California is also home to some of the most stunning national parks: Yosemite, Death Valley, and Joshua Tree. Each park offers stunning landscape views. The national parks offer a diverse environment that ranges from salt flats to sand dunes to badlands to rugged mountains to canyons. Yosemite, Sequoia and Kings Canyon National Parks feature some of the largest trees in the world. In the same parks is the 14,505 foot Mount Whitney, the highest point in the continental United States.

California is also well known for its beaches. North of San Francisco you'll find the Point Reyes National Seashore that was protected in 1962 to set aside one of the last wilderness coastal enclaves. At this park, you'll see an abundance of wildlife ranging from seals to gray whales.

Perhaps second only to the nature of California is the draw of the wine country. Napa Valley has become a popular tourist destination with its range of wineries and world-class restaurants.

SUGGESTED CALIFORNIA RV TRIPS

There are two recommended RV trips in California. One takes you through the Central part of California and the other through the Southern part of California. The first trip in Central California takes you from Ventura to Paso Robles and covers about 161 miles while taking about 3 hours to drive.

Start your trip in Ventura, the ultimate example of a beach town. Here you can enjoy a number of scenic beaches while heading inland to an old-town district. In the harbor, you can go paddle boarding or try one of the unique restaurants along Main Street.

About a half hour away and 34 miles north is Santa Barbara, also known as the "American Riviera." Some popular attractions here include the 18th Century Franciscan Mission Santa Barbara, the Santa Barbara Museum of Art and the Santa Barbara Botanic Garden.

The third stop on this road trip is another hour and a half north, about 83 miles in Pismo Beach. This town is known for its annual Clam Festival along with scenic beaches and tourist attractions. You should stop by the Monarch Butterfly Grove, a eucalyptus grove visited by butterflies in late fall and throughout winter. To the southern edge of town, you'll find the Guadalupe-Nipomo Dunes, the only drive-in beach in central California.

The trip ends forty-five minutes to the north, about 44 miles away in Paso Robles. This town is known for its viticulture industry with several wineries available for tasting. The Paso Robles Pioneer Museum is a popular destination to learn about the settling of the West. This town also features two popular RV parks.

SUGGESTED RV PARKS

The first suggested RV Park is Vines RV Resort. At a total of 125 spaces, this pet-friendly RV park costs $54 to $111 and is open all year. The park features the following amenities:

- ★ Internet
- ★ Restroom and Showers
- ★ Laundry
- ★ RV Supplies
- ★ Ice
- ★ Groceries
- ★ Onsite RV Service
- ★ Cocktail Lounge
- ★ Guest Services
- ★ Heated Pool
- ★ Hot Tub
- ★ Horseshoes
- ★ Recreation Hall
- ★ Pavilion
- ★ Exercise Room

The second suggested RV Park is the Wine Country RV Resort. This park is open all year and costs $54 to $111. It is pet-friendly with 180 spaces and the following amenities:

- ★ Internet
- ★ Restroom and Showers
- ★ Laundry
- ★ RV Supplies

- ★ Metered LP Gas

- ★ Ice

- ★ Groceries

- ★ Onsite RV Service

- ★ Cable

- ★ Cocktail Lounge

- ★ Guest Services

- ★ Heated Pool

- ★ Hot Tub

- ★ Recreation Hall

- ★ Game Room

- ★ Playground

- ★ Pavilion

- ★ Exercise Room

The Southern California RV trip covers about 160 miles and takes about 3 hours. It starts in Malibu and ends in San Diego. The trip starts in Malibu, a favorite surfing and beach destination. The most popular of these is Zuma Beach. Also, El Matador State Beach is known for its sea caves. You can also visit the Getty Villa, filled with art and artifacts from Rome and Greece. A little south of Malibu there is a good RV park to stay at.

SUGGESTED RV PARK IN PLAYA DEL RAY

In the small town of Playa Del Ray, you will find the Dockweiler RV Park. This park is open year-round and costs between $55-$69. It is pet-friendly and has a total of 113 spaces. It comes with the following amenities:

- ★ Restrooms and Showers
- ★ Laundry
- ★ Outdoor Games

The second leg of the trip takes you about 70 miles south on an hour and a half trip to Newport Beach. This is an upscale coastal retreat with plenty of indoor and outdoor activities. Some popular attractions here include the Orange County Museum of Art and the Balboa Island Museum and Historical Society.

The last leg of the trip takes you to San Diego in about an hour and a half for about 90 miles. This is the southernmost city in California and is known for its beaches, Mission-style architecture and cultural attractions. The San Diego Zoo is home to an impressive population of animals as well as the Museum of Man. This area is also home to four wonderful RV parks.

SUGGESTED RV PARKS IN VISTA

First is the Olive Area RV Resort in Vista, CA. This park costs $50 to $65 and is open all year. It is a small park with only 60 total spaces. This pet-friendly park features the following amenities:

- ★ Internet
- ★ Restrooms and Showers
- ★ Laundry
- ★ Cable
- ★ Heated Pool
- ★ Hot Tub

- ★ Recreation Hall

The second RV Park is in Chula Vista as the Chula Vista RV Resort. This large RV Park at 237 spaces comes with its own marina. It is open all year and costs $73 to $95. It is pet-friendly with the following amenities:

- ★ Restrooms and Showers
- ★ Laundry
- ★ ATM
- ★ RV Supplies
- ★ Metered LP Gas
- ★ Ice
- ★ Groceries
- ★ Restaurant
- ★ Cable
- ★ Heated Pool
- ★ Hot Tub
- ★ Horseshoes
- ★ Recreation Hall
- ★ Game Room
- ★ Exercise Room
- ★ Nature Trails
- ★ Bike Rentals
- ★ Putting Green

The third suggested park is Mission Bay RV Resort in San Diego. This park costs $70 to $125 and is open year round. The 260 space, pet-friendly Park features the following amenities:

- ★ Internet
- ★ Restroom and Showers
- ★ Laundry
- ★ RV Supplies
- ★ Firewood
- ★ Ice
- ★ Snack Bar
- ★ Cable
- ★ Horseshoes
- ★ Recreation Hall
- ★ Outdoor Games
- ★ Pavilion

The third and final recommended RV Park is Santee Lakes Recreation Preserve in Santee, CA. At the cost of $48 to $64, this pet-friendly park is open year round and has 300 spaces with the following amenities:

- ★ Internet
- ★ Restroom and Showers
- ★ Laundry
- ★ RV Supplies
- ★ Metered LP Gas
- ★ Firewood
- ★ Ice
- ★ Snack Bar
- ★ Cable
- ★ Fishing Supplies
- ★ Swimming Pool
- ★ Boating

- ★ Hot Tub
- ★ Paddle Boats
- ★ Horseshoes
- ★ Recreation Hall
- ★ Playground
- ★ Outdoor Games
- ★ Pavilion
- ★ Nature Trails
- ★ Pedal Carts
- ★ Bike Rentals

RV CAMPING AT CALIFORNIA STATE PARKS

AMENITIES

- Typical Cost: $7-$195
- Water: Sometimes (23 of 79 parks)
- Electric: Sometimes (23 of 79 parks)
- Sewer: Rare (18 of 79 parks)
- In/Out Rules: Each park has a maximum limit, at which time you have to leave the park for 48 hours. Also, each park has a 30 day maximum per year.

STATE PARKS WITH FULL RV HOOKUPS

- ❏ Woodson Bridge State Recreation Area (132 sites)
- ❏ Folsom Lake State Recreation Area (69 sites)
- ❏ Brannan Island State Recreation Area (102 sites)
- ❏ Lake Del Valle State Recreation Area (150 sites)

- ❏ San Luis Reservoir State Recreation Area (54 sites)
- ❏ Millerton Lake State Recreation Area (148 sites)
- ❏ Dockweiler State Beach (118 sites)
- ❏ Silverwood Lake State Recreation Area (95 sites)
- ❏ Lake Perris State Recreation Area (432 sites)
- ❏ Mount San Jacinto (33 sites)
- ❏ Salton Sea State Recreation Area (48 sites)
- ❏ Providence Mountains State Recreation Area (6 sites)
- ❏ San Clemente State Beach (144 sites)
- ❏ San Elijo State Beach (171 sites)
- ❏ Carpinteria (261 sites)
- ❏ Morro Bay (110 sites)
- ❏ Half Moon Bay (62 sites)

The following state parks have water and electricity only:

- ❏ Bolsa Chica State Beach (57 sites)
- ❏ Crystal Cove (57 sites)
- ❏ San Onofre State Beach (157 sites)
- ❏ Silver Strand State Beach (133 sites)
- ❏ New Brighton State Beach (120 sites)

The following state parks have water and sewage only with no electricity:

- ❏ South Carlsbad State Beach (222 sites)

PRIMITIVE CAMPING SITES IN STATE PARKS

The following state parks are primitive sites only and may only be available seasonally:

- ❏ Jedediah Smith Redwoods (106 sites)
- ❏ Del Norte Coast Redwoods (107 sites)
- ❏ Prairie Creek Redwoods (67 sites)
- ❏ Castle Crags (76 sites)
- ❏ McArthur-Burney Falls Memorial (85 sites)
- ❏ Grizzly Creek Redwoods (18 sites)
- ❏ Humboldt Redwoods (58 sites)
- ❏ Benbow Lake State Recreation Area (46 sites)
- ❏ Richardson Grove (99 sites)
- ❏ Standish-Hickey State Recreation Area (73 sites)
- ❏ Westport-Union Landing State Beach (86 sites)
- ❏ MacKerricher (142 sites)
- ❏ Russian Gulch (30 sites)
- ❏ Van Damme (63 sites)
- ❏ Navarro River Redwoods (26 sites)
- ❏ Hendy Woods (92 sites)
- ❏ Manchester (40 sites)
- ❏ Salt Point (109 sites)
- ❏ Fort Ross State Historic Park
- ❏ Sonoma Coast (90 sites)
- ❏ Sugarloaf Ridge
- ❏ Colusa-Sacramento River State Recreation Area (15 sites)
- ❏ Bidwell-Sacramento River
- ❏ Plumas-Eureka (72 sites)
- ❏ Malakoff Diggins (21 sites)
- ❏ Donner Memorial (154 sites)
- ❏ Ed Z'berg Sugar Pine Point

- ❑ Mount Diablo (36 sites)
- ❑ Caswell Memorial
- ❑ Turlock Lake State Recreation Area (63 sites)
- ❑ McConnell State Recreation Area (15 sites)
- ❑ George J. Hatfield State Recreation Area (20 sites)
- ❑ Henry W. Coe (9 sites)
- ❑ Malibu Creek (63 sites)
- ❑ Chino Hills (24 sites)
- ❑ Doheny State Beach (120 sites)
- ❑ Cuyamaca Rancho (80 sites)
- ❑ Picacho State Recreation Area
- ❑ Emma Wood State Beach (90 sites)
- ❑ El Capitan State Beach (130 sites)
- ❑ Refugio State Beach (67 sites)
- ❑ Gaviota (39 sites)
- ❑ Saddleback Butte (50 sites)
- ❑ Castaic Lake State Recreation Area
- ❑ Red Rock Canyon (50 sites)
- ❑ Pismo State Beach (103 sites)
- ❑ Hearst San Simeon (115 sites)
- ❑ Colonel Allensworth State Historic Park (115 sites)
- ❑ Pfeiffer Big Sur (218 sites)
- ❑ Sunset State Beach (90 sites)
- ❑ Henry Cowell Redwoods (113 sites)
- ❑ Big Basin Redwoods (35 sites)
- ❑ Butano (18 sites)
- ❑ Portola Redwoods (6 sites)

- ❏ Leo Carrillo (135 sites)
- ❏ Point Mugu (68 sites)

COLORADO

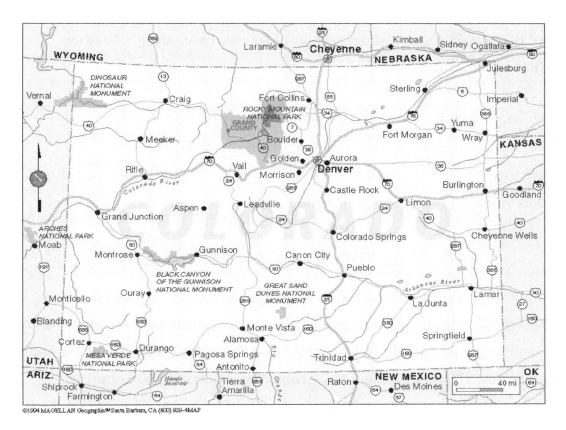

(Credit – Magellan Geography, Santa Barbara, CA)

Colorado is a popular destination for people who enjoy winter sports such as skiing and snowshoeing. However, there is still plenty to do and see in Colorado throughout the rest of the year. Colorado is considered one of the top outdoor states in the United States. There are plenty of opportunities to hike, bike, climb and any other outdoor activity you can think of doing. The Rocky Mountain National Park features over 300 miles of hiking trails and features the Trail Ridge Road; the highest continuous paved road in the United States a 12,000 feet.

For those who want an urban experience, there is the city of Denver. Here you will find a number of cultural sites as well as wonderful dining experiences. Denver is home to many museums focusing on art, science, and history. You can also sample local flavors by visiting a brewery, winery or distillery.

You can also take a step back in time by visiting the town of Durango. Here you can walk through the downtown area that maintains an authentic Old West character. They even have a historic railroad that takes you on a beautiful mountain trip.

SUGGESTED COLORADO RV TRIP

The top RV trip in Colorado is a complete circle from Colorado Springs to Canon City and back to Colorado Springs. This trip takes about six hours and covers 276 miles. Along this trip you get to enjoy the beautiful outdoors while also taking in the history of the Gold Rush and Old West.

Start out in Colorado Springs at the base of the Rocky Mountains at an altitude of 6,000 feet. There are hundreds of miles of trails to hike in this city while also visiting the US Olympic Training Center, the US Air Force Academy and don't forget to visit the Garden of the Gods; a 1,376-acre park featuring towering sandstone formations.

SUGGESTED RV PARK

A good place to stay in Colorado Springs is the Goldfield RV Park. This pet-friendly RV Park is small with only 52 spaces, but it is open year round at a rate of $30 to $41. The park features the following amenities:

- ★ Internet
- ★ Restroom and Showers
- ★ Laundry
- ★ RV Supplies
- ★ Ice
- ★ Onsite RV Service
- ★ Cable

Your trip next takes you about 44 miles to Cripple Creek in about an hour. This two is filled with Old West history as well as a dozen casinos. While there be sure to take a ride on the Cripple Creek and Victor Narrow Gauge Railroad that takes you through the city's historic district. To learn more about the local area, you'll also want to stop by the Cripple Creek District Museum.

The third stop is 96 miles down the road at Saint Elmo and is about a two-hour drive. This town was built around the mining industry and today is one of the best-preserved ghost towns in the United States. Take the time to walk around and explore the old buildings include a schoolhouse, shops and a post office. You can even find a general store that still sells snacks, antiques, and souvenirs.

Another 90 miles takes you to the last stop on the trip, Canon City, in about two hours. This is another former mining town that has preserved its Old West architecture and features the beautiful Colorado Rockies in the background. Here you want to take the time to visit the Royal Gorge Regional Museum and History Center as well as the Prison Museum. While there take a walk across the Royal Gorge Bridge, one of the highest suspension bridges in the world. To complete your trip, you can take the 45 miles, sixty-minute drive back to Colorado Springs.

RV CAMPING AT COLORADO STATE PARKS

AMENITIES

- Typical Cost: $10-$24
- Water: Rarely (10 of 31 parks)
- Electric: Usually (25 of 31 parks)
- Sewer: Rarely (8 of 31 parks)
- Laundry: Occasionally
- In/Out Rules: You are allowed to stay a maximum of 14 days in a 45 day period.

STATE PARKS WITH FULL RV HOOKUPS

- ❏ Chatfield (120 full hookups and 77 electric only)
- ❏ Cherry Creek
- ❏ Cheyenne Mountain
- ❏ James M. Robb Colorado River State Park (17 full hookups, 22 electric only and 12 primitives)
- ❏ Navajo (39 full hookups and 41 electric only)
- ❏ Ridgway (95 full hookups and 187 electric only)
- ❏ Rifle Gap (45 full hookups)
- ❏ Trinidad Lake (6 full hookups and 57 electric only)

The following parks only have electric and water:

- ❏ Crawford State Park (45 sites and 21 primitive sites)

❏ Vega (33 sites and 27 primitive)

The following sites have electric hookups only:

❏ Boyd Lake

❏ Eleven Mile

❏ Golden Gate Canyon (59 sites and 38 primitive)

❏ Jackson Lake

❏ John Martin Reservoir

❏ Lake Pueblo

❏ Lathrop (82 sites and 21 primitive)

❏ Mueller

❏ North Sterling

❏ Rifle Falls

❏ San Luis

❏ Stagecoach

❏ State Forest State Park

❏ Steamboat Lake

❏ Yampa River

PRIMITIVE CAMPING SITES IN STATE PARKS

The following only have primitive campsites:

❏ Arkansas Headwaters Recreation Area

❏ Elkhead Reservoir

❏ Highline Lake

❏ Mancos

❏ Pearl Lake

❏ Sylvan Lake

CONNECTICUT

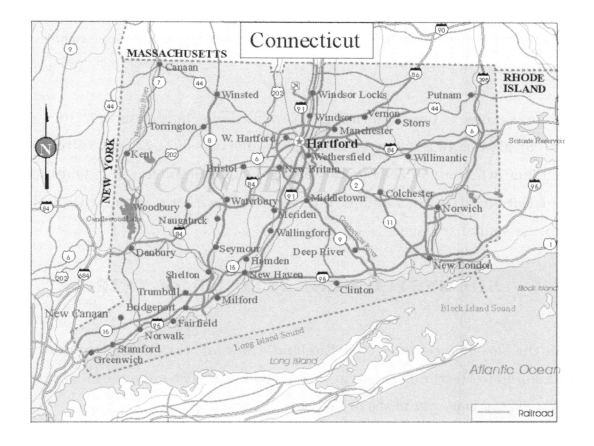

Connecticut is a very small state at just 110 miles from west to east and 70 miles from south to north, but taking an RV trip across it can seem like driving across an entire country. The dramatic and diverse terrain of Connecticut ranges from beaches to towering mountains with thick forests. There is also plenty to see ranging from historic sites to contemporary museums. You can see everything from a Colonial-era town to a thriving modern metropolis.

Along the coast, you will find 253 miles of beach with a number of quaint coastal towns and stunning lighthouses. National Geographic voted

Ocean Beach Park one of the best beaches. On land, you can find a number of scenic hiking trails including Talcott Mountain State Park, which features Heublein Tower. This is a four-story structure built in 1914 to withstand 100-mph winds and today offers panoramic vistas of the surrounding area.

When it comes to towns featuring a New England charm you want to stop by Mystic. In this town you'll find no shortage of historical, cultural and family activities. The Mystic Seaport is a maritime museum features four National Historic Landmark vessels along with a re-created 19th-century seaport village.

SUGGESTED CONNECTICUT RV TRIP

For the best chance to see New England, you want to take the trip from Plainfield to Hartford. This trip covers about 60 miles and takes about an hour. There is plenty to see or do along the way.

Start your trip in the 300 year old town of Plainfield. The city marks the intersection of four major railways from the towns of Hartford, New York, Boston, and Providence. Take a side drive down Old Canterbury Road to the March Route of Rochambeau's Army Historic Site; this will let you see how things were like when the mills were running strong.

The middle stop in your trip is twenty-two minutes away, about eighteen miles from Norwich. This town features a number of beautiful Victorian homes, plus the town features a historic downtown district. The city's harbor sits at the conflux of the Shetucket Thames and Yantic Rivers. To the north, you can visit the Slater Museum, full of art and history.

Your trip ends about fifty minutes and forty miles later in the town of Hartford. This is the capital of Connecticut and has a rich history. Post-Civil War, this was actually the richest city in the United States. You can visit the home and museum of Mark Twain. For outdoor activities, you can walk through the 100-acre Elizabeth Park with a range of trees and plants along with greenhouses, gardens, tennis courts and more.

Connecticut is a small state, and it doesn't take much to drive around. So be sure to venture off this route and see plenty of the other sites Connecticut has to offer. While there consider the top three RV parks to stay at in Connecticut.

SUGGESTED RV PARKS

First is the Seaport RV Resort and Campground in the town of Old Mystic. This park is only open April to October and costs about $46 to $75. Pets are welcome at this 145 space RV Park with the following amenities:

★ Internet
★ Restroom and Showers
★ Laundry
★ RV Supplies
★ Metered LP Gas
★ Firewood
★ Ice
★ Groceries
★ Cable
★ Fishing Supplies
★ Golf Carts

- ★ Heated Pool
- ★ Fishing Pond
- ★ Horseshoes
- ★ Recreation Hall
- ★ Game Room
- ★ Playground
- ★ Outdoor Games
- ★ Pavilion
- ★ Mini Golf

The second option is the Riverdale Farm Campsite in Clinton. This pet-friendly park is open from April to November at the cost of $45 to $50. The park features 250 spaces with the following amenities:

- ★ Internet
- ★ Restroom and Showers
- ★ Laundry
- ★ ATM
- ★ RV Supplies
- ★ Metered LP Gas
- ★ Firewood
- ★ Ice
- ★ Groceries
- ★ Onsite RV Service
- ★ Cable
- ★ Fishing Supplies
- ★ Horseshoes
- ★ Recreation Hall
- ★ Game Room

* Playground
* Outdoor Games
* Pavilion
* Tennis
* Shuffleboard
* Nature Trails

The last option is Hidden Acres Family Campground in Preston. This pet-friendly park has 200 spaces and is open from May to October at the cost of $40 to $58. The park features the following amenities:

* Internet
* Restrooms and Showers
* Laundry
* RV Supplies
* Metered LP Gas
* Firewood
* Ice
* Snack Bar
* Groceries
* Restaurant
* Onsite RV Service
* Fishing Supplies
* Swimming Pool
* Horseshoes
* Recreation Hall
* Game Room
* Playground
* Outdoor Games

★ Pavilion

★ Nature Trails

★ Pickle Ball

RV CAMPING AT CONNECTICUT STATE PARKS

AMENITIES

- Typical Cost: $14-$45
- Water: Rarely
- Electric: Rarely
- Sewer: Never
- In/Out Rules: You can stay for 14 days, then you need to leave for 5 days. Hammonasset Beach and Rocky Neck allow a 21 day stay. Pachaug State Forest, Hopeville Pond, Kettletown and Black Rock State Parks are all considered one park.

CONNECTICUT STATE PARKS

- ❏ Housatonic Meadows Campground (61 sites)
- ❏ Macedonia Brook Campground (51 sites)
- ❏ Lake Waramaug Campground (76 sites)
- ❏ Austin Hawes Campground (30 sites)
- ❏ Black Rock Campground (78 sites)
- ❏ Kettletown Campground (61 sites)
- ❏ Hammonasset Beach Campground (558 sites, some with electric and water)
- ❏ Devil's Hopyard Campground (21 sites)

- Mashamoquet Brook Campgrounds (73 sites, no pets allowed)
- Salt Rock Campground (71 sites, some with electric and water)
- Hopeville Pond Campground (80 sites)
- Pachaug State Forest (40 sites)
- Rocky Neck Campground (160 sites)

DELAWARE

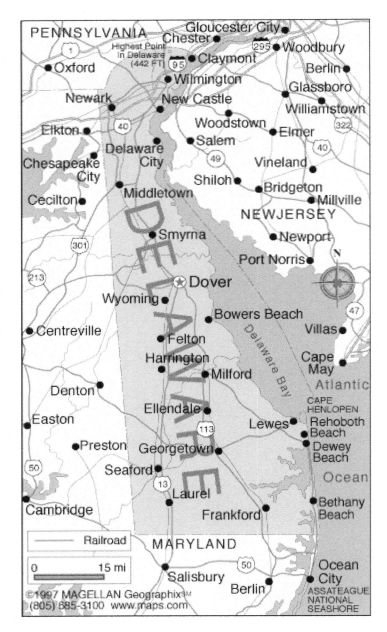

(Credit – www.maps.com)

Delaware is the second smallest state in the United States and is often overlooked by many travelers. However, it can be a wonderful travel destination full of beautiful beaches, rolling hills, extravagant mansions and quaint towns. Throughout the state, you'll find evidence of its rich colonial history in the historic architecture of colonial towns.

In Southern Delaware, you'll find nature that caters to everyone. At Delaware Seashore State Park you'll find six miles of coastline perfect for boaters and surfers. At Cape Henlopen State Park in Lewes, you find an old lighthouse with panoramic views of the coast.

Then there is Rehoboth Beach, which is considered one of the best beaches in the United States because of its boardwalk. It is full of food stands, restaurants, and shopping. There is also the Rehoboth Beach Museum which covers the town's history. In the surrounding area off the boardwalk, you'll find a number of outdoor activities such as kayaking, paddle boarding, sailing and hiking trails.

For those into sports, you can stop at the famous Dover International Speedway, one of the top-rated NASCAR tracks on the east coast. The stadium even has designated RV spots.

SUGGESTED DELAWARE RV TRIP

Delaware may be the second smallest state in the United States, but it is a compact road trip with plenty to see and do. The best road trip starts you in Dover and takes you about 48 miles in about an hour to Rehoboth Beach.

Dover is the historic capital of Delaware with a number of interesting attractions from the Old State House to the Biggs Museum of American

Art with a collection of over 1,800 pieces in 16 galleries. For the sports fans, there is the Dover International Speedway, and music fans can enjoy the annual Firefly Festival. While in Dover there are four main things you can enjoy for free when traveling on a budget.

First, you can visit the Air Mobility Command Museum and see over two dozen aircraft on display. There is also a theater with free movies, flight simulators and a number of exhibits on aviation history. Next, stop by the Delaware State House Museum located on the historic The Green. Third, the Delaware State Police Museum features the history of the state police since 1923 including displays of antique cars and motorcycles. Lastly, if you are traveling during the three day Old Dover Days Festival you'll want to see the pet parade, reenactments, carnival, house tour and plenty of other activities.

The second stop on your road trip is about 50 minutes away in Lewes, a drive of about 41 miles. This town was once a Dutch whaling and trading post that today features several beautiful lighthouses and historical museums. To learn about the local history be sure to visit the Zwaanendael Museum. For an outdoor experience head out to the Cape Henlopen State Park with rugged beaches and a nature center that features aquariums and natural history exhibits.

The final leg of your trip only takes about 22 minutes for the 8-mile drive to Rehoboth Beach. This cute and charming beachfront town has a beautiful boardwalk with shops and restaurants. For the kids, there are plenty of rides and attractions at Funland. Although travelers of all ages can enjoy Gordons Pond, an alternative to the beach with both hiking and bird watching opportunities.

RV CAMPING AT DELAWARE STATE PARKS

AMENITIES

- Typical Cost: $15-$50
- Water: Every park except Lums Pond State Park
- Electric: Every park except Cape Henlopen State Park
- Sewer: Only at Delaware Seashore State Park in warm months
- Laundry: Only at Delaware Seashore State Park
- In/Out Rules: Between Memorial Day and Labor Day, there is a 14 day limit per park. Otherwise, you have a 14-day limit in a 21 day period and can move between parks.

DELAWARE STATE PARKS

- ❏ Cape Henlopen State Park (water only with no hookup sites)
- ❏ Delaware Seashore State Park
- ❏ Killens Pond State Park (water and electric)
- ❏ Lums Pond State Park (electric only)
- ❏ Trap Pond State Park (water and electric)

Known as the Sunshine State, Florida offers visitors weather that often stays on the warm side with some wind and rain. Florida features a number of regions with their own famous attractions. The Panhandle features the Emerald Coast with white sand beaches along the Gulf of Mexico. The northern region is more rural with Old Florida vibes.

Here you will find the largest city in Florida, Jacksonville, and the oldest European settlement, St. Augustine. Central Florida is home to a number of theme parks. The Atlantic Coast is home to the famous Daytona racetrack and the Kennedy Space Center. To the south, you'll find more beautiful coastal towns as well as urban metropolitan cities. Lastly, in the Everglades, you can view a unique ecosystem and some of the most beautiful roadways in the United States that connect to the Florida Keys.

Florida features the most miles of shoreline of any US state. It can be difficult to narrow down your choices and find a beach to visit. You can relax on a beautiful white sand beach, or you can visit South Beach with art deco architecture or the dynamic nightlife scene in Miami. No matter what beach you choose you are sure to enjoy the breathtaking views of the ocean.

In addition to the beautiful beaches, Florida offers a number of public lands to explore nature. The Everglades National Park features 1.5 million acres of wetland wilderness that is home to a number of native plants, alligators, panthers, and flamingos. Throughout the state, you'll be able to explore over 160 state parks with a range of hiking trails and other recreational options.

For those who want a more urban experience, you'll find the southernmost city in the United States, Key West. Here you can experience a Caribbean climate with plenty of restaurants, arts, and music choices. The waters off the shore of the town also offer plenty of adventure options such as diving.

To the northeast, you'll find the historic town of St. Augustine. St. Augustine was started as a Spanish colony in 1565, and you can still see a number of historic structures and stunning architecture.

SUGGESTED FLORIDA RV TRIPS

Florida is a diverse and vast state with a lot of activities to do based on your interests. If you truly want to experience everything this state has to offer, there are three RV trips you should consider. The first takes you along the panhandle portion of Florida in the north. Then as you continue south, the second trip takes you along the gulf shores portion of Florida. The final trip will take you along the southern, Atlantic coast of Florida and Key West. Let's take a look at each of these trips and what you can see along the way as well as some suggested places to stay.

The first trip takes you about five and a half hours through the Florida panhandle from Pensacola to Tallahassee in a trip of about 239 miles. Start your trip in the town of Pensacola located on the Gulf of Mexico. Here you can take a walk through the Pensacola Beach Boardwalk or the Historic Pensacola Village that features a collection of 28 historic buildings. If you are traveling with children, you want to stop by the Children's Museum or the go-kart track at Fast Eddies' Fun Center. While in Pensacola there are two unique things you can do for free.

First is a visit to Fort Barrancas that was built in the 1830s and 1840s to protect the Pensacola Naval Yard. You can either explore the fort on your own or take a guided tour. Be sure to bring flashlights or headlamps as there are some dark tunnels to explore. There are also some nearby picnic tables so you can bring a lunch and enjoy your whole day here.

The second thing is a visit to the Naval Air Station Pensacola, home of the Blue Angels. Most Tuesday and Wednesday mornings you can catch the Blue Angels doing practice maneuvers for free. In addition, you will be able to visit the world's largest naval aviation museum at over 350,000 square feet of everything from biplanes to modern jets with over 150 aircraft on display.

When you are done in Pensacola, take the almost 48-mile drive about an hour east to the town of Destin. This destination is known for its white-sand beaches, and plenty of activities include a range of museums ranging from aviation to fishing. There are also plenty of amusement parks to keep families busy. Here you will also find a recommended RV park.

SUGGESTED RV PARK IN DESTIN

While in the area if you want a place to stay check out the Camp Gulf RV Park in Destin. This 200 space pet-friendly RV Park is open all year at a rate of $85 to $209. It offers you the following amenities:

★ Internet
★ Restroom and Showers
★ Laundry
★ RV Supplies
★ Metered LP Gas
★ Ice
★ Worship Services
★ Cable
★ Fishing Supplies
★ Golf Carts
★ Heated Pool with Water Slide
★ Horseshoes

- ★ Recreation Hall
- ★ Game Room
- ★ Playground
- ★ Outdoor Games
- ★ Pavilion
- ★ Shuffleboard
- ★ Exercise Room
- ★ Bounce Pillow

Your next stop in Panama City is about 55 miles east and takes about an hour and a half to get there. Panama City is the ideal destination for everything water. Take a trip out to Shell Island, a 7-mile long barrier featuring sand dunes, forests, and even its own lake. For families, you want to visit Shipwreck Island Waterpark and the Gulf World Marine Park. For the outdoor adventurer stop by St. Andrews State Park featuring Dr. Beach, consider the best in the region.

Next is a little longer drive of about two hours and 82 miles to the town of Carrabelle. This historic coastal fishing village is a great way to feel like you are stepping back in time to Old Florida. You'll find a number of great beaches as well as some odd roadside attractions such as the World's Smallest Police Station and the Lost Treasure Gallery & Hurricane Museum. While here take a trip out to St. George Island with white-sand beaches and plenty of seashells.

The last leg of your trip is the longest; it takes you about five and a half hours to drive almost 54 miles to the city of Tallahassee. This city is the capital of Florida, and it is a dynamic city with a number of cultural attractions. The outdoor person will enjoy a walk through Alfred B.

Maclay Gardens State Park, and a history buff will enjoy going to the Mission San Luis de Apalachee. However, no trip is complete without visiting the Tallahassee Museum with a number of historic exhibits and walking trails throughout the 52-acre museum.

Once you've finished this RV trip, you can head south for the next suggested trip that takes you along the Gulf Coast. It starts you in the city of Tampa and ends you in the outdoor wonderland of the Everglades. It takes about 4 hours to cover this 219-mile trip. Let's see what sites and places to stay are available to you.

This trip starts you out in the vibrant city of Tampa. Obviously the big attraction here is the Busch Gardens theme park and zoo. However, some smaller attractions include the Riverwalk Area where you can visit the Tampa Museum of Art and the Victorian themed Henry B. Plant Museum.

Next, take the one hour or 60-mile drive to Sarasota. This is a popular white-sand beach destination with plenty of fishing options. If fishing isn't your thing, then explore the Jungle Garden. This ten-acre park features tropical plants and flamingos along with the Marie Selby Botanical Gardens, a research garden featuring thousands of orchids.

SUGGESTED RV PARK IN SARASOTA

Just south of Sarasota you come to a recommended RV park, Sun N Shade RV Resort. This RV Park is located in the small town of Punta Gorda. It is open all year at the cost of $36 to $44. The park is pet-friendly with 191 spaces and the following amenities:

- ★ Internet
- ★ Restrooms and Showers
- ★ Laundry
- ★ RV Supplies
- ★ Ice
- ★ Self-Service RV Wash
- ★ Heated Pool
- ★ Fishing Pond
- ★ Horseshoes
- ★ Recreation Hall
- ★ Outdoor Games
- ★ Shuffleboard
- ★ Nature Trails

From here you'll want to take about an hour and a half drive of about 76 miles south to Fort Myers. This is one of the most popular beach towns in Florida and is the gateway to Sanibel Island. Other popular attractions in the area include the Manatee Springs State Park and the Six Mile Cypress Slough Preserve. For fans of history and architecture, you'll want to visit the Edison and Ford Winter Estates; former homes of two of the biggest icons in the industry.

The next leg of the trip is about 43 miles and takes you almost an hour to get to Naples. This chic town is home to a number of sites. A must see is the Naples Museum of Art, featuring chandeliers made famous by American glassblower Dale Chihuly. Or you can fish from the 19th century Naples Pier. For an outdoor experience, you should head to the Corkscrew Swamp Sanctuary where you'll find the largest old-growth bald cypress trees in the United States. At Naples Zoo and Caribbean

Gardens, you can see 70 endangered species as well as exotic plants from their native habitats. Lastly, you can take a catamaran out to view the primates of Monkey Island located in the middle of an artificial lake. There are several RV parks in Naples that can serve as a staging ground for the last leg of your trip.

The last leg of the trip takes you about an hour to travel the 40 miles to Everglades National Park. This park encompasses 1.5 million acres and is home to the largest subtropical wilderness in the United States and is the second largest national park. You can go fishing or take a guided ranger tour. The best time to visit is in the dry season from December to March. An airboat tour is the best way to experience the park and get to view a number of wildlife such as alligators, bobcats or the endangered Florida panther.

At the southern end of the state, you'll come to the third recommended RV trip. It starts in the city of Melbourne and ends in the islands of Key West. This is the longest trip at just under nine hours and covers 357 miles.

Start your trip in the town of Melbourne, a haven for nature lovers. Take an airboat ride or cruise over to the Brevard Zoo where you can view the animals while paddling a kayak. Another option is to drive to a nearby barrier island and enjoy the Sebastian Inlet, State Park. The nearby Indian River Lagoon features beautiful wetlands. For the family, you can visit Andretti Thrill Park with five go-kart tracks, miniature golf, and laser tag.

The next leg of your trip takes you 49 miles south in about an hour to the town of Fort Pierce. Here you can visit the Navy SEAL Museum or head outdoors at the Teague Hammock Preserve; 300 acres of wetlands featuring cranes, storks, and great blue herons. Outside this town, you'll be able to stay in a suggest RV park before heading off to the next leg of your trip.

SUGGESTED RV PARK IN FORT PIERCE

The Road Runner Travel Resort is located in Fort Pierce. This large park has 452 spaces and is open all year at the cost of $39 to $58. It is pet-friendly and features the following amenities:

★ Internet
★ Restrooms and Showers
★ Laundry
★ ATM
★ RV Supplies
★ Metered LP Gas
★ Firewood
★ Ice
★ Worship Services
★ Groceries
★ Restaurant
★ Self-Service RV Wash
★ Heated Pool
★ Fishing Pond
★ Horseshoes
★ Recreation Hall
★ Game Room
★ Outdoor Games

* Golf
* Tennis
* Shuffleboard
* Putting Green

The next leg of the trip is a long three-hour drive of about 114 miles to the town of Fort Lauderdale. Here you'll find a town that has been nicknamed "Venice of America" for its beaches and boating canals. For a history of the area visit the Old Fort Lauderdale Village and Museum or take in the modern local arts district along the Riverwalk. While here there are three wonderful free things to do. First, you can visit the Old Dillard Museum and learn of the African American heritage in Broward County. Another option is the Plantation Historical Museum that has artifacts from the Seminole and Tequesta tribes or walk through the butterfly garden. Lastly is the Anne Kolb Nature Center with 1,500 acres of mangrove forests and marshes. Just outside of this town there is another RV park you can stay at along this long trip.

SUGGESTED RV PARK IN PARADISE ISLAND

Stop over at the Paradise Island RV Resort. This 232 space park is open all year at a rate of $40 to $50. It's pet-friendly and features the following amenities:

* Internet
* Restrooms and Showers
* Laundry
* RV Supplies

- ★ Ice
- ★ Onsite RV Service
- ★ Self-Service RV Wash
- ★ Heated Pool
- ★ Recreation Hall
- ★ Game Room
- ★ Shuffleboard
- ★ Exercise Room

The second to the last leg of the trip is about 97 miles south but takes about two and a half hours to reach Key Largo. This town is ideal for snorkelers and scuba divers. Here you can visit the first undersea park in the United States, John Pennekamp Coral Reef State Park. Just as you come into town, there is an excellent RV park to stay at.

SUGGESTED RV PARK IN HOMESTEAD

Just before Key Largo, there is the town of Homestead, and here you'll find the Boardwalk RV Resort. This 311 space, pet-friendly Park is open year-round at a rate of $48 to $58 and offers the following amenities:

- ★ Restrooms and Showers
- ★ Laundry
- ★ RV Supplies
- ★ Groceries
- ★ Onsite RV Services
- ★ Guest Services
- ★ Self-Service RV Wash
- ★ Fishing Supplies
- ★ Heated Pool

* ★ Horseshoes
* ★ Recreation Hall
* ★ Playground
* ★ Outdoor Games
* ★ Shuffleboard
* ★ Exercise Room

The last leg of your trip takes you about two hours to drive the 97 miles to Key West. This is the ultimate island getaway. You can visit the Ernest Hemingway house or take in a lot of ocean fun. Snorkel the coral reef, go parasailing, rest up with some fishing or take an eco-tour of the mangroves. In town, you can enjoy a number of museums at the end of this long RV trip.

RV CAMPING AT FLORIDA STATE PARKS

AMENITIES

* Typical Cost: $16-$42
* Water: Always
* Electric: Almost Always
* Sewer: Rarely (8 of 47 parks)
* Laundry: Often
* In/Out Rules: The maximum stay in 14 days, but rangers can extend this to 28 days depending on availability.

STATE PARKS WITH FULL RV HOOKUPS

* ❑ Blackwater River (30 sites)
* ❑ Grayton Beach (59 sites, 21 with sewer)

- ❏ John Pennekamp Coral Reef (47 sites)
- ❏ Myakka River (36 full hookup sites, 77 sites total)
- ❏ Rainbow Springs (47 sites)
- ❏ Suwannee River (30 sites)
- ❏ Topsail Hill Preserve & Gregory E. Moore Resort (156 sites, some with cable)
- ❏ Wekiwa Springs (60 sites, not all are full hookups)

PARKS WITH LIMITED FACILITIES

The following parks have water and electric only:

- ❏ Alafia River (30 sites)
- ❏ Anastasia (139 sites)
- ❏ Bahia Honday (48 sites)
- ❏ Big Lagoon (75 sites)
- ❏ Blue Spring (51 sites)
- ❏ Collier Seminole (120 sites)
- ❏ Curry Hammock (28 sites)
- ❏ St. George Island (60 sites)
- ❏ Falling Waters (24 sites)
- ❏ Faver Dykes (30 sites)
- ❏ Florida Caverns (32 sites)
- ❏ Fort Clinch (64 sites)
- ❏ Fred Gannon Rocky Bayou (42 sites)
- ❏ Gamble Rogers (34 sites)
- ❏ Henderson Beach (60 sites)
- ❏ Highlands Hammock (119 sites)
- ❏ Hillsborough River (112 sites, most with electric)

Finally, the card you deserve with the perks to match.

Thank you for choosing the Southwest Airlines Rapid Rewards® Plus Credit Card from Chase! You're now on your way to earning even more Rapid Rewards® Points, which you can redeem for flights and so much more.

Your new Plus card rewards you with:

▼ **3,000 Anniversary Bonus Points** after your Cardmember Anniversary

▼ **2 Points per $1** spent on all Southwest Airlines purchases

▼ **2 Points per $1** spent on purchases at participating Rapid Rewards Hotel and Car Partners, such as Hyatt, Marriott, Avis, and Hertz

▼ **1 Point per $1** spent on all other purchases

Your Exclusive Cardmember-only benefits:

▼ **Points don't expire as long as your card account is open**, so you can redeem your points

Rapid Rewards® Plus Card Rewards Program Agreement

Important information about this program and this agreement

- Your Rapid Rewards® Plus credit card account is issued solely by JPMorgan Chase Bank, N.A. This Rapid Rewards Plus card rewards program is offered through Southwest Airlines® and Chase. This document describes how the Rapid Rewards Plus card rewards program works and is an agreement between you and Chase. You agree that use of your account or any feature of this program indicates your acceptance of the terms of this agreement. In this document, the following words have special meanings:
  - ◊ "agreement" means this document
  - ◊ "program" means this Rapid Rewards Plus card rewards program
  - ◊ "account" means your credit card account that is linked to this program
  - ◊ "card" means any credit card or account number used to access your account
  - ◊ "we," "us," "our," and "Chase" mean JPMorgan Chase Bank, N.A. and its affiliates
  - ◊ "you" and "your" mean the person responsible for the account and for complying with this agreement
  - ◊ "authorized user" means anyone you permit to use the account
  - ◊ "Rapid Rewards" means the Southwest Airlines Rapid Rewards® program operated by Southwest Airlines Co. and governed by the Rapid Rewards Rules and Regulations, available at **Southwest.com/rrterms**
  - ◊ "purchases" is defined in the section of this agreement titled *How you can earn points*
- Chase may make changes to this program and the terms of this agreement at any time. For example, we may:
  - ◊ add new terms or delete terms
  - ◊ change how you earn points in this program
- Chase may temporarily prohibit you from earning points, using points, using points you've already earned that haven't been transferred to Southwest Airlines, or using any features of this program.
- Chase may supplement this agreement with additional terms, conditions, disclosures, and agreements that will be considered part of this agreement.
- Points earned in this program are automatically transferred to Southwest Airlines after the end of each billing cycle. Southwest Airlines may change the terms of the Rapid Rewards program in accordance with the Rapid Rewards Rules and Regulations.
- This version of the agreement takes the place of any earlier versions, including those that were called "Rewards Program Rules and Regulations." Chase may continue to refer to this agreement as the Rewards Program Rules and Regulations in communications about this program and in supplemental terms, conditions, disclosures, and agreements.

Notice of changes

- You understand that Chase and Southwest Airlines Co. exchange information about you and your accounts and that Southwest Airlines Co. may contact you regarding offers that may be of interest to you.

How you can use your points

- To use your points, go to southwest.com or call Southwest Airlines directly at 1 800 I FLY SWA.

How you could be prohibited from earning or having points transferred

- We may temporarily prohibit you from earning points and we may not transfer points you've already earned to Southwest Airlines:
  - ◊ if you don't make the minimum payment on your account within 30 days of the due date.
  - ◊ if we suspect that you've engaged in fraudulent activity related to your account or this program.
  - ◊ if we suspect you've misused, in any way, the Rapid Rewards program to which points are transferred under this program.
  - ◊ if we suspect that you've misused this program in any way, for example:
    - by repeatedly opening or otherwise maintaining credit card accounts for the purpose of generating rewards
    - by manufacturing spend for the purpose of generating rewards
- You can begin earning points again and any points that we've held will be transferred to Southwest Airlines in the next billing cycle after your account becomes current or when we no longer suspect fraud or misuse of the account or this program.

How you could lose your points

- **You'll immediately lose all points that haven't been transferred to Southwest Airlines if your account status changes, or your account is closed, for any of the following reasons:**
  - ◊ you don't make the minimum payment on your account within 60 days of the due date
  - ◊ you fail to comply with this or other agreements you have with Chase
  - ◊ we believe you may be unwilling or unable to pay your debts on time
  - ◊ you file for bankruptcy
  - ◊ we believe that you've engaged in fraudulent activity related to your account or this program
  - ◊ we believe you've misused, in any way, the Rapid Rewards program to which points are transferred under this program.
  - ◊ we believe that you've misused this program in any way, for example:
    - by repeatedly opening or otherwise maintaining credit card accounts for the purpose

- ❏ Jonathan Dickinson (90 sites)
- ❏ Kissimmee Prairie (35 sites)
- ❏ Koreshan (60 sites)
- ❏ Lake Griffin (40 sites)
- ❏ Lake Kissimmee (60 sites)
- ❏ Lake Louisa (60 sites)
- ❏ Lake Manatee (60 sites)
- ❏ Little Manatee River (30 sites)
- ❏ Little Talbot Island (40 sites)
- ❏ Long Key (60 sites)
- ❏ Manatee Springs (78 sites)
- ❏ Mike Roess (39 sites)
- ❏ O'Leno (61 sites)
- ❏ Ochlockonee River (30 sites)
- ❏ Paynes Prairie (32 sites)
- ❏ Sebastian Inlet (51 sites)
- ❏ Silver Springs (59 sites)
- ❏ Stephen Foster (45 sites)
- ❏ St. Joseph (119 sites)
- ❏ Three Rivers (30 sites)
- ❏ Tomoka (100 sites)
- ❏ Torreya (30 sites)

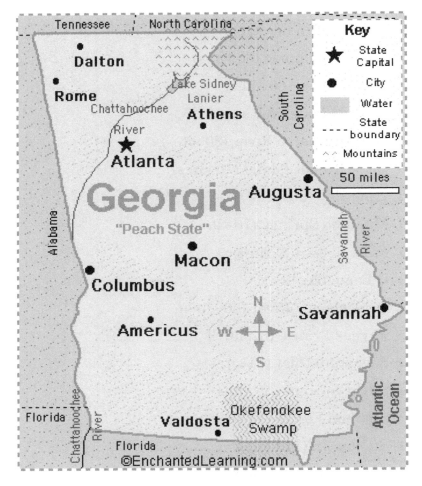

(Credit – www.enchantedLearning.com)

Georgia was the last of the original 13 colonies and is a pivotal point in American history. The state also offers a stunning range of natural beauty from the Blue Ridge Mountains in the north to the beautiful ocean views in the south. Atlanta offers a metropolitan landscape for those who want an urban experience filled with Southern culture, unique cuisine, and hospitality.

For the outdoor adventurer, you want to visit Northern Georgia, known by the Cherokee as the "Land of a Thousand Waterfalls." Here you will find three of the highest waterfalls in the eastern United States. The Chattahoochee River offers plenty of adventures when it comes to rafting, kayaking or canoeing.

Savannah is not only the oldest city in Georgia but also possibly the prettiest. The historic style and hospitality in this city make it a very relaxing retreat. For a more modern urban experience, you want to visit Atlanta. Here you will find a number of sports arenas, museums, theaters and family attractions, so you are sure to find something to keep you busy.

SUGGESTED GEORGIA RV TRIPS

There are two excellent RV trips to take in the state of Georgia. The first takes you through the central part of the state while the second takes you along the Atlantic coast. Each offers a variety of sites to see and a few good options for staying overnight.

The first trip is a loop that takes you through central Georgia. It starts in the capital of Atlanta and circles around to Columbus before heading back to Atlanta. The trip can take about eight and a half hours to cover 520 miles.

Start your trip in Atlanta, a sprawling city. Here you'll find a number of Civil War-era and Civil Rights Movement-related sites along with a number of modern activities and cultural scenes. Some popular sites include the Georgia Aquarium, the World of Coca-Cola and the Martin

Luther King Jr. National Historic Site. Just thirty minutes from downtown you'll find a suggested RV park.

SUGGESTED RV PARK MCDONOUGH

The Atlanta South RV Resort is in the small town of McDonough. This pet-friendly RV Park has 170 spaces and is open all year round with rates of $40 to $50 with the following amenities:

- ★ Restrooms and Showers
- ★ Laundry
- ★ RV Supplies
- ★ Metered LP Gas
- ★ Firewood
- ★ Ice
- ★ Self-Service RV Wash
- ★ Swimming Pool
- ★ Recreation Hall
- ★ Playground
- ★ Pavilion

The next stop on the trip is Macon about 84 miles south and takes about an hour. This compact city is known for its historic homes and musical heritage. Two major attractions are the Otis Redding Foundation and the Allman Brothers Band Museum at the Big House. You'll also want to visit the Tubman Museum, the largest African-American museum in the area. Also, there is the Georgia Sports Hall of Fame, the largest sports museum in the state.

Next, you'll continue 105 miles south for about an hour and a half to the town of Tifton. This small town is characterized by historic homes and excellent fishing options. The Tifton Residential Historic District and the Georgia Museum of Agriculture & Historic Village are two great ways to experience the past. You will be able to see a traditional farm, a rural town and a museum that focuses on the history of agriculture.

The shortest leg of the trip is about 48 minutes away and about 49 miles to the small town of Valdosta. This city is known for Wild Adventures, a zoo and theme park with a giraffe feeding zoo. There is also plenty to do art lovers, particularly the Annette Howell Turner Center for the Arts.

The final leg of your trip takes you about an hour and a half to drive the 175 miles to Columbus. Here you can visit the 40,000 square foot National Civil War Naval Museum featuring artifacts and dioramas. You'll even be able to see the CSS Chattahoochee and the hull of the largest remaining Confederate warship, the CSS Jackson. Along the Chattahoochee River, you can take advantage of a raft tour. You can stay at a local RV park before closing the loop with the nearly two hours, 108-mile drive back to Atlanta.

SUGGESTED RV PARK IN COLUMBUS

The Lake Pines RV Park and Campground is a smaller site with 112 spaces. It costs $40 and is open all year round. This pet-friendly park features the following amenities:

★ Restrooms and Showers
★ Laundry
★ Metered LP Gas

- ★ Firewood
- ★ Ice
- ★ Guest Services
- ★ Self-Service RV Wash
- ★ Swimming Pool
- ★ Fishing Pond
- ★ Horseshoes
- ★ Recreation Hall
- ★ Playground
- ★ Outdoor Games
- ★ Nature Trails

The second trip in Georgia takes you along the Atlantic Coast. It starts out in Brunswick and ends in Tybee Island. The trip only takes about two hours and covers about 97 miles. Start your trip in Brunswick, the known capital of shrimp. This town dates back to the colonial era and retains the configuration of the British settlers. There are a number of festivals to take advantage of throughout the years.

Take the short 17-mile drive to Darien in about 27 minutes. This city lies within one of the largest estuarine systems in the world. Here you will be surrounded by natural beauty and well-preserved historic buildings. A must see if the R.J. Reynolds Mansion from 1810 on Sapelo Island. There are also plenty of water activities in the area.

Your next stop is about 62 miles away in Savannah and takes about an hour to get there. This port town is one of the most beautiful cities in the American South. In the famous historic district, you'll find a number of 18th and 19th-century buildings. There is plenty of attractions to see and do around this town. Plus there is a nice RV park to stay at.

In Savannah, you'll find the Savannah Oaks RV Resort. This pet-friendly RV Park even features an enclosed dog run. There are 139 sites in this park that is open all year at the cost of $44 to $49 and features the following amenities:

- ★ Internet
- ★ Restrooms and Showers
- ★ Laundry
- ★ RV Supplies
- ★ Metered LP Gas
- ★ Firewood
- ★ Ice
- ★ Snack Bar
- ★ Groceries
- ★ Onsite RV Service
- ★ Cable
- ★ Fishing Supplies
- ★ Swimming Pool
- ★ Boat Ramp
- ★ Boat Rental
- ★ Paddle Boats
- ★ Horseshoes
- ★ Game Room
- ★ Playground
- ★ Exercise Room

The last stop on this trip is Tybee Island, 41 minutes and about 18-mile drive east. This is a popular Atlantic coast destination for families. Here you can do a number of outdoor activities such as cycling, kayaking or just relax on the beach. A popular attraction is the Tybee Island Light Station, the oldest and tallest lighthouse in Georgia.

You can even climb 178 steps to the panoramic deck at the top. Two other popular attractions are the Marine Science Center and the historic Fort Pulaski that dates back to the Civil War.

RV CAMPING AT GEORGIA STATE PARKS

AMENITIES

- Typical Cost: $23-$43
- Water: Always
- Electric: Always, except recreational areas out of season
- Sewer: Rarely (5 out of 42 parks)
- Laundry: Usually (At full hookup parks and resorts)
- In/Out Rules: There are no maximum stay restrictions

STATE PARKS WITH FULL HOOKUPS

- ❏ Florence Marina (43 sites)
- ❏ Gordonia-Alatamaha (29 sites)
- ❏ Little Ocmulgee (64 sites)
- ❏ Reed Bingham
- ❏ Unicoi State Park (40 sites, plus water & electric only sites)

PARK WITH LIMITED FACILITIES

The following parks have water and electric hookups only:

- ❏ A.H. Stephens (42 sites)

- ❏ Amicalola Falls (24 sites)
- ❏ Black Rock Mountain (66 sites)
- ❏ Bobby Brown State Outdoor Recreation Area (61 sites, only in season)
- ❏ Chattahoochee Bend (51 sites)
- ❏ Cloudland Canyon (98 sites)
- ❏ Crooked River (72 sites)
- ❏ Don Carter (56 sites)
- ❏ Elijah Clark (165 sites)
- ❏ F.D. Roosevelt (162 sites)
- ❏ Fort McAllister (65 sites)
- ❏ Fort Mountain (70 sites)
- ❏ Fort Yargo (61 sites)
- ❏ General Coffee (58 sites)
- ❏ George L. Smith (30 sites)
- ❏ Georgia Veterans Memorial (77 sites)
- ❏ Hamburg State Outdoor Recreation Area (30 sites, seasonal)
- ❏ Hard Labor Creek (79 sites)
- ❏ Hart State Outdoor Recreation Area (61 sites, seasonal)
- ❏ High Falls (106 sites)
- ❏ Indian Springs (70 sites)
- ❏ James H. (Sloppy) Floyd (25 sites)
- ❏ Kolomoki Mounds (26 sites)
- ❏ Laura S. Walker (44 sites)
- ❏ Magnolia Springs (34 sites)
- ❏ Mistletoe (102 sites)
- ❏ Moccasin Creek (54 sites)
- ❏ Red Top Mountain (111 sites)
- ❏ Richard B. Russell (27 sites)

- ❏ Seminole (46 sites)
- ❏ Skidaway Island (87 sites)
- ❏ Stephen C. Foster (48 sites)
- ❏ Tallulah Gorge (50 sites)
- ❏ Tugaloo (100 sites)
- ❏ Victoria Bryant (24 sites)
- ❏ Vogel (56 sites)
- ❏ Watson Mill Bridge (32 sites)

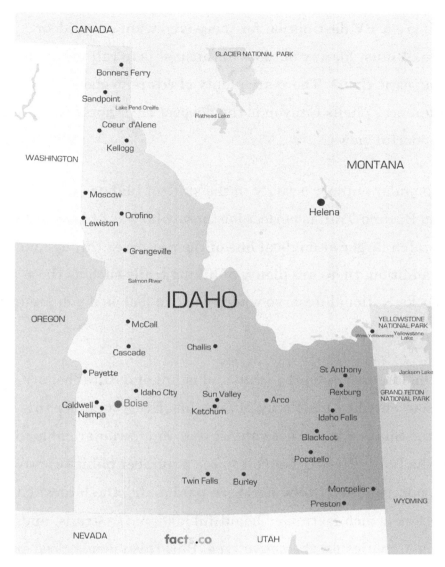

(Credit- www.facts.com)

Idaho is home to epic expanses of a landscape filled with pine tree filled mountains, huge waterfalls, and rushing rivers. The state is home to over 100 mountain ranges with the eastern skyline being dominated by the

Rocky Mountains. Among all this natural beauty you'll also find bustling cities such as Boise, Idaho Falls, and Coeur d'Alene.

Idaho is a great RV destination for those who want an outdoor adventure. A must for any outdoor enthusiast is to raft down one of Idaho's majestic rivers. There are plenty of rivers to choose from based on your preferences. Hells Canyon is the deepest river gorge in America and offers wonderful views.

Another popular outdoor activity in the state of Idaho is wildlife viewing. The Idaho Birding Trail is perfect for those who want to watch birds. Or you can watch larger animals at one of the preserves throughout the state. In addition, there are plenty of hiking trails such as those at the City of Rocks National Reserve where you can feel as if you are hiking in the sky.

Boise is the largest city in the state and is full of natural beauty. The skyline is accented by the Rocky Mountains. Every summer this city is home to the Shakespeare Festival. All year round you are able to stroll through the Boise River Greenbelt to see a number of historic stops and cultural opportunities. In the northern panhandle, the largest city is Coeur d'Alene which features a beautiful lake, parks, trails, and number of sporting activities for the active type. Plus this town is close enough to Montana and Washington to provide a few day trip options.

East of Boise a wonderful and unique stop is the Craters of the Moon National Monument and Preserve. Here you will see a rugged landscape that is like the surface of another world. This is because of the ancient lava flows. Nearby, the town of Arco features the world's first nuclear power plant. Just a little farther south is the Shoshone Falls, nicknamed the Niagara Falls of the West; which are actually higher than the actual Niagara Falls.

SUGGESTED IDAHO RV TRIP

The best RV trip to take will allow you to cover the heart of Idaho and all it has to offer. Start your trip in the capital of Boise and end in the town of McCall. This short 106-mile trip will only take you about two hours to complete.

Your trip starts out in the largest city of Boise. Despite it being a metropolis, the main attractions are still the outdoors. A must see, the World Center for Birds of Prey, where you can learn all about the raptor species in the wild. For the adults, the town offers several distilleries and breweries to enjoy.

Continue your trip 76 miles north to the town of Cascade; it takes about an hour and a half. This town is located on the southeast shore of Lake Cascade and is the perfect spot to stay if you want to explore the surrounding forests and mountains. For the adventurous person visit Kelly's Whitewater Park where you can kayak some controlled rapids.

The last leg of your trip takes you thirty miles north to McCall in about a half hour. This town presents you with miles of hiking and exploring options at the 1,000-acre Ponderosa State Park. In the winter months, you can take advantage of a number of snowshoe and cross-country skiing options.

RV CAMPING AT IDAHO STATE PARKS

AMENITIES

- Typical Cost: $12-$45
- Water: Usually (only one park has no water)
- Electric: Usually (only one park has no electric)
- Sewer: Often (9 out of 16 parks)

IDAHO STATE PARKS

- ❑ Henry's Lake (8 full hookups, 58 water & electric, 17 electric only)
- ❑ Lake Walcott (22 water & electric, 18 primitive)
- ❑ Massacre Rocks (41 water & electric)
- ❑ City of Rock National Reserve (64 sites)
- ❑ Castle Rocks (37 water & electric)
- ❑ Three Island Crossing (1 full hookup, 63 water & electric, 18 shared sites)
- ❑ Bruneau Dunes (81 water & electric, 31 primitive sites)
- ❑ Lake Cascade (36 full hookups, 16 water & electric, 5 shared sites, 4 water only, 11 primitive shared sites, 41 primitive sites)
- ❑ Ponderosa (40 full hookups, 10 shared full hookup sites, 89 water & electric, 23 shared sites)
- ❑ Winchester Lake (2 full hookups, 42 water & electric, 2 shared sites, 22 primitive sites)
- ❑ Hells Gates (11 full hookups, 50 water & electric, 29 primitive sites)
- ❑ Heyburn (15 full hookups, 41 water & electric, 71 primitive sites)
- ❑ Farragut (5 full hookups, 140 water & electric, 16 shared sites, 6 primitive shared sites, 55 primitive sites)

❏ Round Lake (16 water & electric, 35 primitive sites)

❏ Priest Lake (11 full hookups, 62 water & electric, 78 primitive sites)

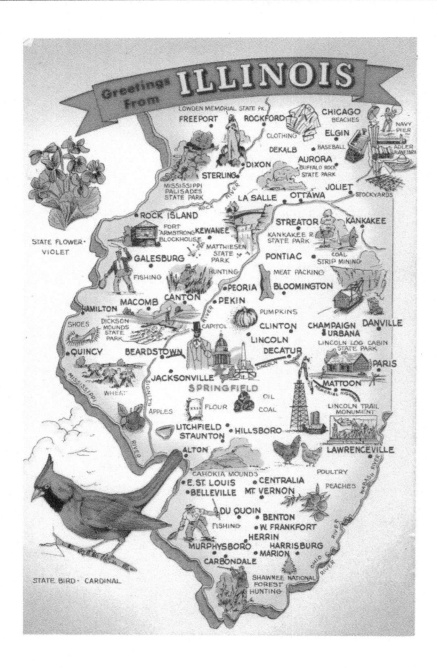

Most think of Chicago when they think about the state of Illinois. The state is actually a contrast, it has endless expanses of farms in the south and then a skyline of skyscrapers in the north along the border of Lake

Michigan. In between, there is a number of rural towns and prairies. There is always something to meet your pace in Illinois.

Starting just west of the city of Chicago, there are plenty of scenic outdoor spots in Illinois. Starved Rock State Park features towering sandstone walls with beautiful waterfalls. To the south of the state, there is the Shawnee National Forest full of beautiful green hills and rugged landscapes. Then there are the wetlands of the Cache River State Natural Area that features unique flora and fauna in a constantly flooded forest. For human-made nature, there is Rockford's Nicholas Conservatory and Anderson Japanese Gardens.

For an urban experience, there is obviously Chicago that is packed with a number of adventures. North Michigan Avenue has a stretch known as the Magnificent Mile filled with towering skyscrapers. From Willis Towers Skydeck you can enjoy stunning views. For sports fan, you must visit the historic Wrigley Field.

For those who are fans of history, you need to visit the Land of Lincoln. Near Springfield, you will find a number of sites that preserve the history of Abraham Lincoln. You can visit his former home, law office, and the old capitol building. Some good places to visit include the Abraham Lincoln Presidential Library and the New Salem State Historic Site featuring a replica of the type of village Lincoln lived in the 1830s.

SUGGESTED ILLINOIS RV TRIP

When traveling by RV to Illinois, there is a recommended trip that will take you from the big city in Chicago to the small country towns of

Caledonia and Galena. In total the trip takes about four and a half hours, covering 263 miles. Let's take a look at what you can see on this trip.

Start your trip in the big city of Chicago, with enough sites to keep you busy all day; if not several days. In fact, there are eight free things that you should do to enjoy the full spectrum of what the city has to offer. First, you want to visit the Lincoln Park Zoo. This is one of only three zoos in the United States that is free. You can visit tropical rainforests, reptile houses, exotic birds, and mammals. You can even observe training and feeding sessions at certain times of the day.

Next, head to the Garfield Park Conservatory; something even the locals don't know about. This is free and has a variety of educational activities throughout the year. The last Wednesday of the month includes animal activities and scavenger hunts. Then there is the most popular tourist attraction in Chicago, Navy Pier. This 3,300-foot long pier extends out into Lake Michigan. There is a variety of things to see and do along this pier, including free activities.

Fourth, is a visit to the Chicago Children's Museum. There is a realistic firehouse kids can play in, plus an urban garden with insects and flowers. You can also visit a recreation of a 1997 expedition to the Sahara desert to unearth dinosaurs. There is plenty of activities to keep the children busy all day. Another option is to head for Millennium Park where you can enjoy free concerts in the summer and ice skating in the winter. Visit the Field Museum for free on the second Monday of each month and see a range from dinosaur bones, a pueblo, animals and science activities.

Located in the Pilsen neighborhood, you can visit the largest Latino cultural organization, the National Museum of Mexican Art. Lastly, for the art enthusiast, you can also visit the Art Institute of Chicago with an impressive collection of Impressionist and post-Impressionist artwork. For the kids, there is even art-making activities and games.

The second leg of the trip will take you about three hours to get the 164 miles to the town of Caledonia. This town is a few miles from the Wisconsin border and is known for the McEachran Homestead Winery, the only one in Boone County. This historic farm encompasses 285 acres, 11 of which are dedicated to growing 19 different varieties of grapes and fruit trees.

The last leg of the trip takes you about two hours to drive 99 miles to Galena Cellars. This is located in the northwest corner of the state and is home to the Galena Cellars Vineyard, a two-time winner of the Illinois' Winemaker of the Year award. This vineyard grows 22 types of grapes and 40 different varieties of wine.

RV CAMPING AT ILLINOIS STATE PARKS

AMENITIES

- Typical Cost: $8-$35
- Water: Sometimes
- Electric: Almost always
- Sewer: Rarely
- Laundry: Rarely
- In/Out Rules: 14 days maximum in a 30 day period with a 5 day advanced reservation required.

ILLINOIS STATE PARKS

- ❏ Pere Marquette State Park (80 electric only sites)
- ❏ Lincoln Trail State Park (240 water & electric sites)
- ❏ Horseshoe Lake Recreation Area (38 water & electric sites, 50 electric only sites and 10 primitive sites)
- ❏ Kickapoo State Recreation Area (90 electric sites, 90 primitive sites)
- ❏ Jubilee College State Park (108 electric only sites)
- ❏ Sam Parr State Park (10 electric only sites)
- ❏ Stephen A. Forbes State Park (115 water & electric sites)
- ❏ Eldon Hazlet State Recreation Area (328 water & electric sites)
- ❏ Walnut Point State Park (34 electric only sites)
- ❏ Fox Ridge State Park (42 electric only sites)
- ❏ Moraine View State Recreation Area (132 electric only sites)
- ❏ Beaver Dam State Park (59 electric only sites)
- ❏ Jim Edgar Panther Creek Wildlife Area (82 full hookup sites)
- ❏ Hidden Springs State Forest (primitive sites only)
- ❏ Ramsey Lake State Park (90 electric only sites)
- ❏ Clinton Lake State Recreation Area (231 sites, including full hookups)
- ❏ Wolf Creek State Park (80 sites, including full hookups)
- ❏ Eagle Creek State Park (380 electric only sites)
- ❏ Weldon Springs State Park (77 electric only sites)
- ❏ Sangchris Lake State Park (197 electric only sites)
- ❏ Wayne Fitzgerrell State Park (243 electric only sites)
- ❏ Sam Dale Lake State Fish and Wildlife Area (68 electric only sites)
- ❏ Red Hills State Park (100 water & electric sites)
- ❏ Lake Murphysboro State Park (61 electric only sites)

- Hamilton County State Fish and Wildlife Area (60 electric only sites)
- Giant City State Park (85 water & electric sites)
- Fort Massac State Park (50 electric only sites)
- Ferne Clyffe State Park (36 electric only sites)
- Apple River Canyon State Park (50 primitive sites)
- Argyle Lake State Park (86 electric only, plus primitive sites)
- Illini State Park (99 electric only sites)
- Johnson-Sauk Trail State Recreation Area (70 electric only sites)
- Lake Le-Aqua-Na State Recreation Area (108 electric only sites)
- Lowden State Park (80 electric only sites)
- Mississippi Palisades State Park (110 electric only sites, 131 primitive sites)
- Morrison-Rockwood State Park (92 electric only sites)
- Prophetstown State Park (159 sites, some full hookups)
- Rock Cut State Park (210 electric only sites)
- Shabbona Lake State Recreation Area (150 electric only sites)
- Starved Rock State Park (129 electric only sites)
- White Pines State Park (3 electric only sites)
- Illinois Beach State Park (241 electric only sites)
- Chain O'Lakes State Park (151 electric only sites, plus primitive sites)
- Kankakee River State Park (160 electric only sites)
- Nauvoo State Park (150 electric only sites)
- Randolph County State Recreation Area (59 electric only sites)
- Siloam Springs State Park (98 electric only sites)
- Washington County State Recreation Area (37 electric only sites)
- Weinberg State Fish & Wildlife Area (19 electric only sites)
- Dixon Springs State Park (50 water & electric sites)

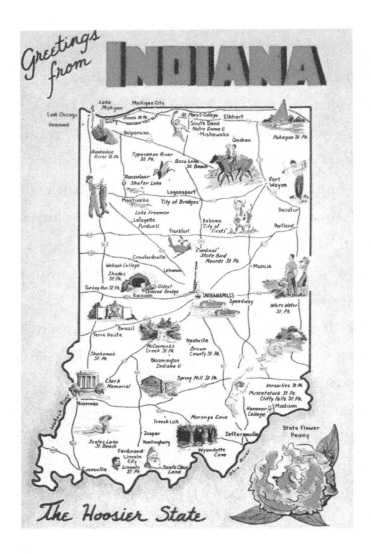

Perhaps one of the most interesting facts about Indiana is the fact that the majority of American RVs are built in the town of Elkhart and the surrounding area. Elkhart is also home to the RV/MH Hall of Fame with some interesting history about recreational travel. Of course, there is plenty of other things to see and do in Indiana.

For sports fans, a must stop is the University of Notre Dame in South Bend. To the south is the Indy 500, which attracts about 300,000 visitors a year. You'll also find a number of smaller communities and beautiful natural areas. There is plenty of wonderful outdoor experiences in Indiana.

When you think of Indiana, you don't automatically think if sand dunes and waterfalls, but you'll find both in this state. The Indiana Dunes National Lakeshore takes up 15,000 acres in the northwest section of the state and features four ecosystems of dunes, prairies, woodlands, and wetlands.

For an urban experience, there is plenty to do in Indianapolis. The best way to see the most sites is to take the Cultural Trail. This gives you the opportunity to visit a number of eclectic neighborhoods and historic sites. You can also see the town by floating down the Central Canal in a gondola.

SUGGESTED INDIANA RV TRIP

The suggested Indiana RV trip takes you through the heart of the state to see everything it has to offer from big city to small town. Start out in Monticello and end in Clarksville on a 286-mile journey that takes you about five and a half hours. Let's see what you have to look forward to on this trip.

Start your trip in the town of Monticello, popular for its lakes and family-friendly activities. The most popular attraction is the Indiana Beach Boardwalk Resort; an amusement and waterpark with plenty of activities for the whole family. If you are interested in swimming or boating, you should head to Lake Shafer or Freeman. In the evening, take advantage of one of the few remaining drive-in theaters in the state.

The second leg of your trip takes you to Indianapolis, about 85 miles south, in about two hours. Indianapolis is best known as the location of the annual Indy 500, but there is plenty else to do throughout the year. For the outdoor adventurer, there is the White River State Park, a 250-acre green space with a concert venue, a botanical garden, the Indianapolis Zoo and a few museums; the best of which is the Eiteljorg Museum of American Indians and Western Art. While in Indianapolis there are four free activities you can enjoy.

First, is the world's best children's museum; the Children's Museum of Indianapolis. It is one of the largest children's museum in the United States. Recently they even opened a permanent outer space themed exhibit. Another option for the whole family is to visit the Arts Garden. This is a glass-enclosed structure attached to the Circle Centre Mall. Here you can take part in over 300 free activities for the whole family. The structure itself is impressive at seven-stories tall and suspended 17 feet above the intersection of Washington and Illinois Streets.

The third option is a stop by the National Art Museum of Sport. Here you'll find a range of art inspired by sports and sports figures. Lastly, you can visit the Garfield Park Conservatory featuring over 500 tropical plant varieties and a 15-foot waterfall. There is even the Sunken Gardens, a showcase of three acres of European classical formal gardens.

Once you are done enjoying everything in Indianapolis, head on down the road to the small town of Rising Sun. It is a moderate drive of about two hours and 111 miles. This little town is set along the Ohio River and is mostly known as the Rising Star Casino Resort; which even has an attached RV park you can stay at. There is plenty to see and do even if you don't want to gamble including a golf course, entertainment options, and a buffet.

SUGGESTED RV PARK

The Rising Star Casino Resort and RV Park is an excellent stop along your trip. It is open all year at a rate of $40 to $70. However, this pet-friendly park is small at only 56 spaces. You will be able to enjoy the following amenities:

- ★ Internet
- ★ Restrooms and Showers
- ★ Laundry
- ★ ATM
- ★ Ice
- ★ Snack Bar
- ★ Restaurant
- ★ Cable
- ★ Cocktail Lounge
- ★ Guest Services
- ★ Swimming Pool
- ★ Golf
- ★ Pavilion
- ★ Sauna
- ★ Shuffleboard
- ★ Exercise Room

The last leg of the trip will take you about an hour and a half to drive about 81 miles to the town of Clarksville right across the river from Louisville, Kentucky. The most popular attraction here is the Falls of the Ohio State Park with its exposed fossil beds dating back to the Paleozoic Devonian Era. There is also a number of flower gardens and river access.

RV CAMPING AT INDIANA STATE PARKS

AMENITIES

- Typical Cost: $10-$40
- Water: Not Usually
- Electric: Almost Always
- Sewer: Rarely (4 out of 33 parks)
- In/Out Rules: A maximum stay is 14 days. Also, Thursday through Sunday the minimum requirement is two nights.

INDIANA STATE PARKS

- ❏ Brookville Lake State Park (62 full hookups, 388 electric only)
- ❏ Brown County State Park (401 electric only, 28 primitive sites)
- ❏ Cagles Mill Lake / Lieber State Recreation Area (120 electric only, 96 additional sites)
- ❏ Cecil M. Harden Lake / Raccoon State Recreation Area (240 electric only)
- ❏ Chain O'Lakes State Park (331 electric only, 82 primitive sites)
- ❏ Charlestown Lake (60 full hookups, 132 electric only)
- ❏ Clifty Falls (106 electric only, 63 primitive sites)
- ❏ Hardy Lake (149 electric only, 18 primitive sites)

- Harmonie (200 electric only)
- Indiana Dunes (140 electric only)
- J. Edward Roush Fish and Wildlife Area (25 electric only, 67 primitive sites)
- Lincoln State Park (150 electric only, 111 primitive sites)
- McCormick's Creek (189 electric only, 32 primitive sites)
- Mississinewa Lake (39 full hookups, 335 electric only, plus primitive sites)
- Monroe Lake (226 electric only, 94 primitive sites)
- Mounds (75 electric only)
- O'Bannon Woods (281 electric only, 25 primitive sites)
- Ouabache (124 electric only)
- Patoka Lake (455 electric only, 45 primitive sites)
- Pokagon State Park / Trine State Recreation Area (220 electric only, 73 primitive sites)
- Potato Creek (287 electric only)
- Prophetstown (55 full hookups, 55 electric only)
- Lost Bridge West State Recreational Area (245 electric only, 38 primitive sites)
- Salamonie River State Forest (36 primitive sites)
- Shades State Park (105 primitive sites)
- Shakamak (122 electric only, 42 primitive sites)
- Spring Mill (187 electric only, 36 primitive sites)
- Summit Lake (73 electric only)
- Tippecanoe River (112 electric only)
- Turkey Run (213 electric only)
- Versailles (226 electric only)
- Whitewater Memorial (236 electric only, 35 primitive sites)

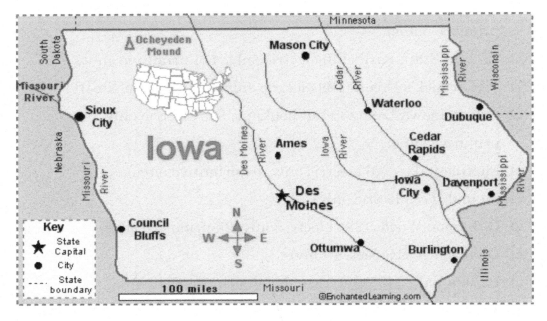

(Credit – www.EnchantedLearning.com)

Iowa is the center of the American heartland, where you find wide-open spaces and friendly people. The major geographic feature of the state is the Missouri and Mississippi Rivers that form two of the borders. The rest of the state is filled with several lakes and rivers surrounded by rolling hills and dense forests. Among all the nature are charming small towns and bustling cities.

The Okoboji region of Iowa is known as the Iowa Great Lakes. Here you will find 12,000 acres of beautiful, glacier-carved lakes. These lakes offer excellent fishing opportunities. You'll also find a number of state parks in the area with options such as beaches, boating, hiking and plenty of other recreational opportunities.

In the central part of the state, you find the capital city of Des Moines which offers plenty of attractions. You can visit the beautiful gold-capped Capitol building, the Pappajohn Sculpture Park, and the Downtown Farmers Market. If you are visiting in August, you need to stop by the Iowa State Fair.

For the historical inclined you should stop by the Amana Colonies. This area of Iowa was built up by German settlers in the mid-1800s and has maintained its architecture and history. You'll also find plenty of authentic culinary experiences at any of the bakeries, breweries or restaurants.

SUGGESTED IOWA RV TRIP

To experience both the history and breathtaking views of Iowa you want to take an RV trip that follows the mighty Mississippi River. Start out in the town of Burlington and end in Dubuque. This a relatively short trip of 176 miles that only takes about four hours to drive, but has a ton of stuff to see and do along the way.

Start your trip out in the historic town of Burlington that was settled in 1805 on bluffs overlooking the mighty Mississippi River. This town soon developed into a river port filled with steamboats and railroads. Pretty much anywhere you walk in this town; you'll find buildings listed on the National Register of Historic Places. For a unique experience check out Snake Alley, the world's most crooked alleyway.

Next head north to the metro area of Iowa at Quad Cities. This trip is about 78 miles and takes almost two hours. This metro area actually encompasses four cities in two states, brought together by the mighty Mississippi River. At one time this area was about the riverboat traffic, but today there are plenty of interesting roadside attractions to visit including the world's largest truck stop, visiting the botanic center or attending a concert. You can even take a cruise on the Mississippi River aboard the 750-passenger Celebration Belle paddleboat for a unique experience.

Continue north and end your trip in the town of Dubuque. This town allows you to enjoy beautiful building architecture along with the scenes of the Mississippi River. At the Shot Tower, you can see how bullets were cast throughout history. Or you can take a walk through the Arboretum and Botanical Gardens. Take the Fourth Street Elevator for a ride up and down the bluffs of the Mississippi on the shortest and steepest railroad in the world. Also, don't miss out on visiting the National Mississippi River Museum and Aquarium.

RV CAMPING AT IOWA STATE PARKS

AMENITIES

- Typical Cost: $13-$16
- Water: Sometimes
- Electric: Almost Always (only two parks don't have electric)
- Sewer: Sometimes (11 out of 46 parks)
- In/Out Rules: Two-week maximum stay with three days before return.

Iowa State Parks

- ☐ Backbone (108 sites)
- ☐ Beeds Lake (135 sites)
- ☐ Black Hawk (126 sites)
- ☐ Brushy Creek (37 sites, 8 full hookups)
- ☐ Clear Lake (177 sites, 7 full hookups)
- ☐ Dolliver Memorial (20 sites)
- ☐ Elk Rock (30 sites)
- ☑ Emerson Bay State Recreation (82 sites, 24 full hookups)
- ☐ Geode (87 sites)
- ☐ George Wythe (47 sites)
- ☑ Green Valley (63 sites, 15 full hookups)
- ☐ Gull Point (60 sites)
- ☐ Honey Creek (103 sites, 28 full hookups)
- ☐ Lacey-Keosauqua (54 sites)
- ☐ Lake Ahquabi (75 sites)
- ☑ Lake Anita (92 sites, 40 full hookups)
- ☐ Lake Darling (37 sites)
- ☐ Lake Keomah (37 sites)
- ☑ Lake Macbride (43 sites, 11 full hookups)
- ☐ Lake of Three Fires (24 sites)
- ☐ Lake Wapello (40 sites)
- ☐ Ledges (40 sites)
- ☐ Lewis and Clark (106 sites, 13 full hookups)
- ☐ Maquoketa Caves (17 sites)
- ☐ Marble Beach State Recreation Area (102 sites)
- ☐ McIntosh Woods (45 sites)
- ☐ Nine Eagles (27 sites)

- ❏ Palisades-Kepler (18 sites)
- ❏ Pikes Peak (52 sites)
- ❏ Pilot Knob (48 sites)
- ❏ Pine Lake (97 sites)
- ❏ Pleasant Creek (55 sites)
- ❏ Prairie Rose (77 sites, 8 full hookups)
- ❏ Red Haw (58 sites)
- ❏ Rock Creek (98 sites)
- ❏ Shimek Forest Campground (37 primitive sites)
- ❏ Springbrook (73 sites)
- ❏ Stephens Forest Campground (25 sites, no electricity)
- ❏ Stone (8 sites)
- ❏ Union Grove (7 full hookups)
- ❏ Viking Lake (20 sites)
- ❏ Volga River State Recreation Area (72 sites, 32 full hookups)
- ❏ Walnut Woods (22 sites, 9 full hookups)
- ❏ Wapsipinicon (13 sites)
- ❏ Waubonsie (61 sites, 36 primitive)
- ❏ Wildcat Den (28 sites, no electricity)
- ❏ Wilson Island (78 sites)

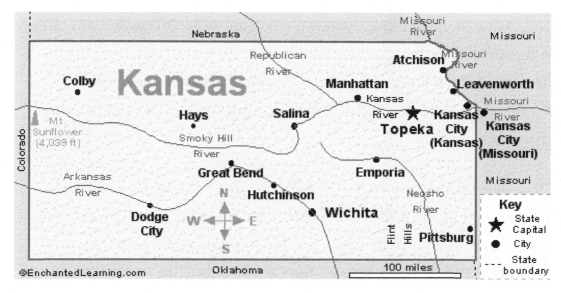

(Credit – www.EnchantedLearning.com)

Kansas is the epitome of the American heartland. Throughout the state, you'll find remnants of the Wild West history. However, there is a lot more to the state than history. You'll find a number of aviation attractions, art galleries, and outdoor activities.

There is no better place for outdoor activity than Kansas. The state is home to some of the best hunting in the United States since its diverse landscapes offer a range of game species. The state is home to 300,000 acres of public lands and over a million acres of private lands that are open for seasonal hunting of deer, turkey, antelope, pheasants and more.

Kansas also offers plenty of hiking opportunities that cover cliffs, waterfalls and rolling hills. The best trail for views is the Tallgrass

Prairie National Preserve in Flint Hills. You may even find a glimpse of a bison herd.

Once you're done outdoors, you can enjoy one of the many vibrant cities in Kansas. Wichita is the largest city and features 33 museums, 22 attractions, 22 live theaters and 17 festivals. Top choices are the Botanica gardens, the Wichita Grand Opera and the Kansas Aviation Museum.

Then there is the town of Topeka which is home to the Combat Air Museum, the Kansas Museum of History and the popular Topeka Zoo. Two top attractions in this city are the Strataca or the Kansas Underground Salt Museum and the Cosmosphere; the second-largest space museum in the United States.

SUGGESTED KANSAS RV TRIP

The trip isn't long in Kansas, but it gives you another world to visit. Start out in Kansas City and drive to Wamego, while going through the Land of Oz. The trip is 106 miles and only takes about two hours, but that gives you plenty of time to take in the sights.

Start your trip out in the town of Kansas City. Here you can step back in time at the Arabia Steamboat Museum featuring frontier-era artifacts. The Arabia is a steamboat that carried 200 tons of goods to stores along the Missouri River when it sank in 1856. The steamboat was excavated with remarkably preserved artifacts that you can enjoy today. You won't find this much history at any other museum.

Follow the paths of wagon trains as you head west for an hour or about 62 miles to get to the town of Topeka. Take the time to enjoy all that the state capital has to offer, including some excellent canoeing and kayaking options on the Kansas River.

You can also visit the Combat Air Museum or the Kansas Museum of History. For a chance to see living history, head to the Old Prairie Town for a look at frontier lifestyles. Head over to Gage Park to see how the city played a part in the Civil Right Movement and ride on an original 1908 carousel.

The last leg of your trip only takes you 43 miles west to the town of Wamego in about forty minutes. Visit this town to see the world-famous Oz Museum with its over 25,000 artifacts and memorabilia from the 1939 film. There is also a number of Oz themed attractions throughout the town and an annual celebration in October.

RV CAMPING AT KANSAS STATE PARKS

AMENITIES

- Typical Cost: $12-$15
- Water: Always
- Electric: Always
- Sewer: Sometimes (13 of 23 parks)
- In/Out Rules: 14 days maximum, can be extended another 14 with written permission from a park ranger. Must stay out 5 days before returning.

KANSAS STATE PARKS

- ❏ Cedar Bluff (16 full hookups, 102 water & electric, 20 electric only)
- ❏ Cheney (222 water & electric)
- ❏ Clinton (205 water & electric)
- ❏ Crawford (38 water & electric, 28 electric only)
- ❏ Cross Timbers (19 full hookups, 50 water & electric, 8 electric only)
- ❏ Eisenhower (37 full hookups, 81 water & electric, 68 electric only)
- ❏ El Dorado (165 full hookups, 307 water & electric)
- ❏ Elk City (14 full hookups, 85 water & electric)
- ❏ Fall River (44 water & electric)
- ❏ Glen Elder (107 water & electric)
- ❏ Hillsdale (180 water & electric)
- ❏ Kanopolis (15 full hookups, 53 water & electric, 63 electric only)
- ❏ Meade (42 water & electric)
- ❏ Lovewell (28 full hookups, 78 water & electric, 49 electric only)
- ❏ Milford (51 full hookups, 90 water & electric)
- ❏ Perry (110 water & electric)
- ❏ Pomona (41 full hookups, 93 water & electric)
- ❏ Prairie Dog (13 full hookups, 60 water & electric)
- ❏ Sand Hills (44 full hookups, 20 water & electric)
- ❏ Scott (7 full hookups, 50 water & electric)
- ❏ Tuttle Creek (8 full hookups, 159 water & electric, 44 electric only)
- ❏ Webster (82 water & electric, 10 electric only)
- ❏ Wilson (99 water & electric, 37 electric only)

KENTUCKY

Kentucky is a state known for its horses and bourbon. However, it is also a state where caverns stretch for miles underground, cities teem with activity, and towering hills provide plenty of outdoor adventures. No matter what your interests you'll find something in Kentucky to do while RV traveling.

When it comes to national parks, Kentucky is second to none. The Daniel Boone National Forest in the southeast part of the state spans 706,000 acres and some 21 counties. Within the park boundaries, there are over 600 miles of roads and trails.

Then there is the Cumberland Gap National Historical Park featuring just as much history as scenery. This national park is also home to a number of wildlife and underground caves. Lastly, there is Mammoth Cave National Park; which has the longest cave system in the world.

Perhaps one of the biggest attractions in Kentucky is the famous Kentucky Derby at Churchill Downs Racetrack in Louisville in May. The race may only last two minutes, but the entire event takes two-weeks.

East from Louisville is the city of Lexington, which is the horse capital of the world and is home to a 1,200 acre Kentucky Horse Park. The second biggest draw to Kentucky is the Bourbon Trail that consists of nine distilleries.

SUGGESTED KENTUCKY RV TRIP

Kentucky offers a range of indoor and outdoor activities, with this ideal RV trip you can experience the best of everything Kentucky has to offer. It takes you 332 miles from the town of Paducah to the city of Lexington in about five and a half hours. Let's see what you can enjoy on this unique trip.

Start your trip in the town of Paducah, known for its arts and architecture by being designated a UNESCO Creative City. The town is also known for its quilting culture and features the National Quilt Museum. Other points of interest to consider is the Paducah Symphony Orchestra, the Maiden Alley Cinema, and Gallery and the Yeiser Art Center. If you want to spend some time outdoors, consider walking around the 20-block historic district with prime examples of Victorian homes.

The next stop 186 miles away is the Cave City and it takes about three hours to get there. This is your gateway to Mammoth Cave National Park, the longest cave system in the world. There is plenty of other activities to do above ground as well. For the outdoor individual, you can bike, canoe or go horseback riding. The city features an impressive three zip lines within a five-mile radius of the town.

Continuing about 120 miles along your journey, in about two hours you reach Frankfort. As the capital of Kentucky, this town has plenty of historic sites, perhaps the most popular is the grave of Daniel Boone. The State Capitol Building is also home to the Capital City Museum that shows you the history of Kentucky through the centuries. Be sure to stop by the Buffalo Trace Distillery, a National Historic Landmark and offering Bourbon tastings.

SUGGESTED RV PARK

If you need a place to stay consider the Elkhorn Campground in Frankfort. This 125 space, pet-friendly RV Park costs $34 and is open all year long with the following amenities:

- ★ Internet
- ★ Restrooms and Showers
- ★ Laundry
- ★ RV Supplies
- ★ Metered LP Gas
- ★ Firewood
- ★ Ice
- ★ Worship Services
- ★ Groceries

- ★ Cable
- ★ Fishing Supplies
- ★ Swimming Pool
- ★ Horseshoes
- ★ Recreation Hall
- ★ Game Room
- ★ Playground
- ★ Outdoor Games
- ★ Pavilion

The last leg of your trip is a short 26-mile drive to Lexington of about 43 minutes. This is considered the heart of Kentucky and the horse capital of the world. There are two major race tracks here: Keeneland and The Red Mile. Be sure to visit the Kentucky Horse Park with a museum and horse farm for retired racehorses. In addition, there are a few other free things to enjoy while in Lexington.

When you visit Keeneland Thoroughbred Racing, you will be able to watch early morning workouts and take a self-guided tour of the track. Head to the Raven Run Nature Sanctuary and explore 734 acres of hiking trails through the natural beauty of meadows, woodlands, and streams. For more outdoor experiences visit the Lexington Convention and Visitors Bureau where you can get a tour map for walking or driving through historic Lexington, plus you can schedule a free horse farm tour.

For indoor experiences consider the Lexington History Museum, the only free historic site in Lexington. It is located in the former Fayette County Courthouse and provides you with a variety of exhibits and activities. Take a tour through Old Kentucky Chocolates to see how candy is made and enjoy a few samples. Lastly, head to Camp Nelson National Cemetery and Civil War Site where you can hike over five miles of interpretive trails through an old Civil War base.

RV CAMPING AT KENTUCKY STATE PARKS

AMENITIES

- Typical Cost: $17-$35
- Water: Always
- Electric: Always
- Sewer: Sometimes (13 out of 31 parks)
- Laundry: Often at resort parks
- In/Out Rules: 14 day maximum, but can be extended with permission from a park ranger.

KENTUCKY STATE PARKS

The following state parks are open year-round:

- ❏ Carter Caves (89 full hookups)
- ❏ Columbus-Belmont (37 full hookups)
- ❏ Fort Boonesborough (167 full hookups)
- ❏ General Butler (111 full hookup)
- ❏ Kentucky Horse Park (260 water & electric)
- ❏ Levi Jackson (135 full hookups)
- ❏ Paintsville Lake (32 full hookups)

The following state parks open on April 1st and close around October/November:

- ❑ Barren River Lake (98 sites, some with full hookups)
- ❑ Big Bone Lick (60 water & electric)
- ❑ Blue Licks Battlefield (49 water & electric)
- ❑ Carr Creek (38 water & electric)
- ❑ Cumberland Falls (89 water & electric)
- ❑ Dale Hollow Lake (145 full hookups)
- ❑ General Burnside Island (100 water & electric)
- ❑ Grayson Lake (69 water & electric)
- ❑ Green River Lake (157 water & electric)
- ❑ Greenbo Lake (92 full hookups)
- ❑ Jenny Wiley (117 water & electric)
- ❑ John James Audubon (75 water & electric)
- ❑ Kenlake (60 water & electric)
- ❑ Kentucky Dam Village (221 water & electric)
- ❑ Kincaid Lake (84 water & electric)
- ❑ Lake Barkley (79 water & electric)
- ❑ Lake Cumberland (50 full hookups)
- ❑ Lake Malone (26 water & electric)
- ❑ My Old Kentucky Home (39 full hookups)
- ❑ Natural Bridge (109 full hookups)
- ❑ Nolin Lake (32 water & electric)
- ❑ Pennyrile Forest (100 water & electric)
- ❑ Taylorsville Lake (70 water & electric)
- ❑ Yatesville Lake (47 full hookups)

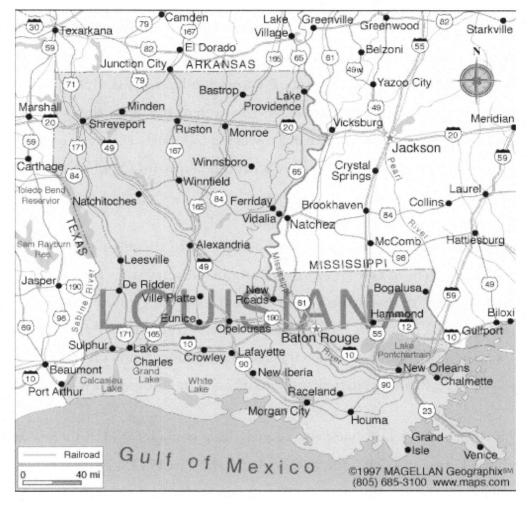

(Credit – www.maps.com)

Louisiana has an energy all to itself. The northern half of the state is full of diverse towns, and the southern portion of the state features colorful Creole and Cajun parishes. Throughout history, Louisiana has been a colony of Spain and France until becoming a part of the United States. All of these cultures have left marks on the state.

The state parks in Louisiana offer plenty of outdoor activities. In the heel of Louisiana, there is Sam Houston Jones State Park, the perfect destination for bird lovers. Here you will have a chance to see over 200 species of birds throughout the year. Similarly, South Toledo Bend State Park gives you the opportunity to see nesting bald eagles. In the toe of the state, you'll find Tickfaw State Park with a boardwalk that takes you through four different ecosystems. At the arch of the state there is Jungle Gardens on Avery Island featuring towering oak trees covered in Spanish moss. Lastly, there is Lake Charles with the beautiful Creole Nature Trail.

No trip to Louisiana is complete without a visit to the most famous city of New Orleans. There is a bit of everything in this city from the vibrant French Quarter to the solemn quiet of the Lafayette Cemetery and the National WWII Museum. You can visit the city any number of ways, but it is worth your time to see the city from a steamboat ride on the Mississippi or through historic neighborhoods in a horse-drawn carriage.

If you want a more laid-back city to visit then consider Natchitoches in northern Louisiana. This town was established in 1714, nearly a century before Louisiana became a state. This town is the best example of antebellum. Nearby, you'll find the Cane River National Heritage Area which showcases the natural and cultural elements of the area.

SUGGESTED LOUISIANA RV TRIP

Nothing beats authentic Louisiana culture and cuisine. Take a 303-mile loop of about six hours to get the best of everything Louisiana has to offer. Start the trip in Lafayette, the capital of Cajun Country. Here you'll be able to experience the rhythms and flavors of Cajun. If you are there on a Friday afternoon, be sure to catch a street dance known as fais-do-do. Also be sure to try some genuine Cajun cuisine while here.

Take a short 37-minute drive about 21 miles down the road to New Iberia. This small and historic town is known as the home of Tabasco Sauce. However, you can also check out Shadows-on-Teche; a beautiful antebellum mansion. Or perhaps you would rather walk through the 200-acre Jungle Gardens. Although if you only have time for one thing while in this town, head out to Avery Island to see how Tabasco Sauce is made.

Continue about an hour and a half down the road to Houma, about 84 miles away. This town has a popular bayou with plenty of boat tour options so you can view alligators, pelicans, and turtles in their natural habitat. There are also plenty of museums to visit in this town, but the best is the Bayou Terrebonne Waterlife Museum about local life and history. For birdwatching, be sure to stop by the Mandalay National Wildlife Refuge.

Next, head to the most popular city of New Orleans about 57 miles away or a drive of about an hour. This city is easily a must visit for anyone in Louisiana. Here you'll view charming neighborhoods ranging from the Garden District to the French Quarter. Also be sure to try the popular cuisine of the area.

SUGGESTED RV PARKS

Within New Orleans, you can stay at Jude Travel Park of New Orleans. It is open all year at a rate of $30 to $65. This pet-friendly RV Park is small with only 46 spaces. It offers you the following amenities:

- ★ Internet
- ★ Restrooms and Showers
- ★ Laundry
- ★ Ice
- ★ Guest Services
- ★ Swimming Pool
- ★ Hot Tub
- ★ Pavilion

Just outside of New Orleans in the town of Slidell you can enjoy Pine Crest RV Park of New Orleans. It is open all year at a rate of $36 to $40. It is pet-friendly with a total of 202 spaces and the following amenities:

- ★ Internet
- ★ Restrooms and Showers
- ★ Laundry
- ★ Metered LP Gas
- ★ Ice
- ★ Recreation Hall
- ★ Playground
- ★ Pavilion
- ★ Shuffleboard

The last leg of the trip takes you to Baton Rouge. It is about 81 miles and takes you about an hour and a half to get there. The capital city of Louisiana is the place to go to try the authentic cuisine of both Cajun and Creole variety. You can try spots on your own or take one of the many food tours available in the city. Once you've had your fill, you can close the loop by driving about an hour or 60 miles back to Lafayette.

RV CAMPING AT LOUISIANA STATE PARKS

AMENITIES

- Typical Cost: $18-$28
- Water: Always
- Electric: Always
- Sewer: Rarely (only 4 parks have full hookups)
- In/Out Rules: Maximum 14-night stay.

LOUISIANA STATE PARKS

- ❑ Bayou Segnette State Park (99 sites)
- ❑ Beaver Dam Campground (27 sites)
- ❑ Bogue Chitto State Park (81 full hookups)
- ❑ Chemin-A-Haut State Park (26 sites)
- ❑ Chicot State Park (198 sites)
- ❑ Fairview-Riverside State Park (81 sites)
- ❑ Fontainebleau State Park (107 sites, 4 full hookups)
- ❑ Grand Isle State Park (49 sites)
- ❑ Hodges Gardens State Park (9 primitive sites)
- ❑ Jimmie Davis State Park (73 sites)
- ❑ Lake Bistineau State Park (67 sites)
- ❑ Lake Bruin State Park (47 sites)
- ❑ Lake Claiborne State Park (85 sites)
- ❑ Lake D'Arbonne State Park (65 sites)
- ❑ Lake Fausse Pointe State Park (50 sites)
- ❑ North Toledo Bend State Park (62 sites)
- ❑ Palmetto Island State Park (96 sites)

- ❏ Poverty Point Reservoir State Park (54 sites, many with full hookups)
- ❏ Sam Houston Jones State Park (75 sites, some with full hookups)
- ❏ South Toledo Bend State Park (55 sites)
- ❏ St. Bernard State Park (51 sites)
- ❏ Tickfaw State Park (30 sites)

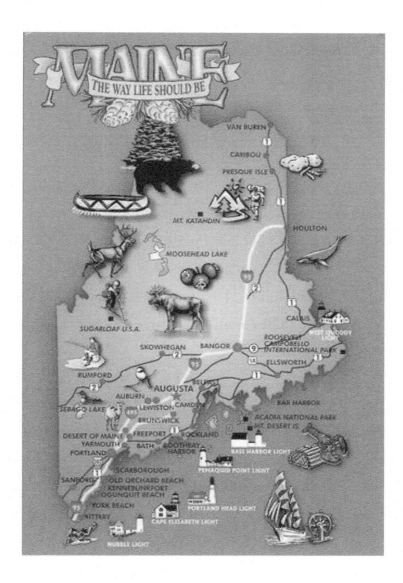

Maine is state of unsurpassed beauty. The majority of the state is filled with a rugged wilderness. The eastern coast has small towns and a few larger population centers, most of which boom with visitors during the summer.

Maine is home to the oldest national park east of the Mississippi and takes up 47,000 acres along the coast. Acadia National Park provides plenty of outdoor activity options including hiking, bicycling and wildlife viewing. Nearly 300 miles of the Appalachian Trail passes through Maine and provide plenty of day hiking options, but be prepared since the trails in this state are known for their particularly challenging terrain.

For the urban traveler, the largest city in Maine is Portland. Visit the Old Port District to step back in time with cobblestone streets and historic buildings. You can visit the Portland Observatory for views overlooking the city. There are plenty of cultural experiences to enjoy as well. Then there is the ultimate seaside town of Kennebunkport that was established in the 1600s. This town has both a historic area as well as plenty of entertainment areas.

Take a drive along the coast, and you will be able to view a number of historic lighthouses while taking advantage of a number of whale-watching opportunities. You can even charter a boat to take you out on the water to see whales, dolphins, and seals in the wild. You can also take a kayak and canoe tour to view the moose in its natural habitat.

SUGGESTED MAINE RV TRIP

Maine is a stunning state, and no RV trip is complete without taking in the stunning coast and beautiful lighthouses that dot it. A 205-mile drive from York to Bar Harbor will take you along the majority of the southern coast of Maine in about four and a half hours.

Start your trip in the southeastern corner of the state in the town of York. This is one of the oldest cities in the United States. It features beautiful old houses, a beautiful harbor and a two-mile long stretch of beach. Visit the Museums of Old York to see a series of historic buildings that date for centuries. No visit is complete without a visit to the Nubble Lighthouse, one of the most photographed lighthouses in the world.

The second leg of the trip is a quick 18 minutes' drive of about 50 miles to the town of Wells. This town is famous for its antique stores, fresh-catch seafood, and beautiful beaches. You can spend an entire day browsing through over 25 antique shops. If you'd rather spend your time outdoors, then head over to the Rachel Carson National Wildlife Refuge, a 50 miles long beach with plenty of bird watching and hiking options.

The third stop is another short 35 minutes down the road in Portland, about 24 miles away. Portland is the largest city in Maine and is one of its most popular tourist destinations. Most people come for the Old Port Exchange, a historic district still featuring cobblestoned streets and historic buildings. You can also find a number of restaurants offering traditional New England clam chowder and a number of lobster dishes. You'll also find a number of lighthouses in the area, six of them within a 20-minute drive of town.

Next, you'll take a little longer trip of about two hours to cover the 80 miles to Camden. This is a popular spot for a summer getaway, and the harbor is often full of yachts. You'll find plenty of boating and swimming options in Lake Magunticook. You can also take the time to walk around the Old World-style historic district. If you are traveling in the summer, you'll want to stay for the Camden Windjammer Festival for a weekend of festivities and fireworks.

The final leg of the trip takes you about an hour and a half to travel about 58 miles to Bar Harbor. This town is located on Maine's Mount Desert Island. In the warmer months, this is a popular outdoor travel destination with a number of hiking and biking trails in Acadia National Park. In town, there is a number of boutiques, farmers markets and museums to keep you busy for a while.

RV CAMPING AT MAINE STATE PARKS

AMENITIES

- Typical Cost: $10-$40
- Water: Sometimes
- Electric: Rarely
- Sewer: Never
- In/Out Rules: 14 night stay maximum from the last Saturday in June to the third Saturday in August. Outside this time there is no maximum limit, but you can only reserve 14 days at a time.

MAINE STATE PARKS

- ❑ Aroostook State Park (30 primitive sites)
- ❑ Bradbury Mountain State Park (35 primitive sites)
- ❑ Camden Hills State Park (107 water & electric)
- ❑ Cobscook Bay State Park (106 primitive sites)
- ❑ Lake St. George State Park (22 electric only sites)
- ❑ Lamoine State Park (62 primitive sites)

- Lily Bay State Park (100 primitive sites)
- Mount Blue State Park (136 primitive sites)
- Peaks-Kenny State Park (56 primitive sites)
- Rangeley Lakes State Park (50 primitive sites)
- Sebago Lake State Park (250 water & electric)
-

MARYLAND

(Credit –www.EnchantedLearning.com)

Known as the Old Line State, Maryland is home to many possibilities ranging from the pristine beaches in the east to the towering Appalachian Mountains in the west. There is such variety in Maryland that it is said you can see American just by traveling through Maryland. You can see natural landscapes, visit historic attractions, enjoy urban cities and walk through quaint towns.

When it comes to an outdoor adventure, you should look no further than Maryland's portion of the Appalachian Trail. The trail covers 40 miles in Maryland from Pen Mar to the Potomac River and takes you through historic sites as well as scenic overlooks. Two of the most popular day hikes along this trail is Greenbrier State Park to Annapolis Rocks and from Gathland State Park to Weverton Cliffs.

Another popular outdoor activity is fishing along the Savage River. This waterway covers 30 miles and is regularly stocked with rainbow trout in the upper river and wild brown or brook trout in the lower river. On the Chesapeake Bay, you can try you had at catching some crabs with no permit required. If you would rather just watch the wildlife head to the nearby Blackwater National Wildlife Refuge with 26,000 acres of forest, marshes, and ponds housing a number endangered species such as Delmarva Peninsula fox squirrels and a number of migratory birds.

If the beach is more your thing, then there are plenty of art scene, food culture, historic neighborhoods and museums along the harbors and beaches of Maryland. There is no better plan than the Inner Harbor of Baltimore. Here you will find brick pathways that take you to a number of parks, restaurants, and shops. Some popular attractions in this area including the National Aquarium, the American Visionary Art Museum, and the Maryland Science Center.

Another popular option is to the south at Annapolis. Here you can visit a rich naval heritage and beautiful views of the Chesapeake Bay. In the summer months, both tourists and locals typically head for Ocean City with its three-mile boardwalk that runs parallel to the beaches and features a variety of attractions. For a more relaxed atmosphere head to Assateague State Park on Assateague Island where you can find a variety of watersports or view the famous wild horses.

SUGGESTED MARYLAND RV TRIP

Maryland is a state of charming towns, beautiful coastline and plenty of recreational options. To experience all of this you'll want to take an RV trip from Ocean City to Woodbine, covering 195 miles along the way in about five hours driving time.

Your trip started in Ocean City, known for its 3 miles long boardwalk that features shops, restaurants, and amusement attractions. This boardwalk dates back to 1902. Another must-see attraction is Assateague Island just south of town where you can see a large herd of wild ponies as well as diverse species of birds.

A short journey of 30 miles that takes about 42 minutes gets you to the second destination of Salisbury. Take the time to walk around Salisbury Zoological Park that focuses on species conservation. You can also go to Pemberton Historical Park; the centerpiece of this 262-acre historical site is Pemberton Hall that dates back to 1741. For adults, there are a number of microbreweries and pubs to enjoy.

SUGGESTED RV PARK IN GREENSBORO

On your way to your third stop, you can choose to stay at Holiday Park Campground in the town of Greensboro. This park is open from April to November and costs $43 to $57. This pet-friendly RV Park features an enclosed dog run as well as 190 spaces with the following amenities:

★ Internet
★ Restrooms and Showers
★ Laundry
★ RV Supplies
★ Metered LP Gas
★ Firewood
★ Ice

- ★ Worship Services
- ★ Snack Bar
- ★ Groceries
- ★ Cable
- ★ Swimming Pool
- ★ Horseshoes
- ★ Recreation Hall
- ★ Game Room
- ★ Playground
- ★ Outdoor Games
- ★ Pavilion
- ★ Tennis
- ★ Shuffleboard
- ★ Nature Trails

Your next destination is Rock Hall, about 55 miles away or a drive of about an hour. This waterfront community has been nicknamed "The Pearl of the Chesapeake." You'll find a number of top seafood restaurants as well as sailing and fishing options. Take advantage of the number of walking and biking paths that provide you with a range of scenic ocean views.

Next, you'll drive about two hours or 110 miles to Woodbine. This rural town gives you a chance to relax in nature, but still be within minutes of an urban center. There are a few wineries listed among the top wineries on the East Coast. You'll also be able to enjoy plenty of side trips to nearby Baltimore and Washington D.C.

SUGGESTED RV PARK IN FREDERICKSBURG

If you need a place to stay while taking advantage of all the side trips, then consider stopping in at Ramblin' Pines Family Campground and RV Park. This 200 space park is pet-friendly and open year round at a rate of $63 with the following amenities:

- ★ Internet
- ★ Restrooms and Showers
- ★ Laundry
- ★ RV Supplies
- ★ Metered LP Gas
- ★ Firewood
- ★ Ice
- ★ Groceries
- ★ Fishing Supplies
- ★ Heated Pool
- ★ Fishing Pond
- ★ Horseshoes
- ★ Recreation Hall
- ★ Game Room
- ★ Playground
- ★ Pavilion
- ★ Shuffleboard
- ★ Exercise Room
- ★ Nature Trails
- ★ Bounce Pillow
- ★ Mini Golf

RV CAMPING AT MARYLAND STATE PARKS

AMENITIES

- Typical Cost: $23-$50
- Water: Rarely (2 out of 20 parks)
- Electric: Usually (only 3 parks are primitive)
- Sewer: Rarely (only at Point Lookout State Park)
- In/Out Rules: 14 night maximum.

MARYLAND STATE PARKS

- ❏ Assateague State Park (350 sites, some with electric)
- ❏ Big Run (29 primitive sites)
- ❏ Cedarville State Forest (30 electric sites)
- ❏ Cunningham Falls (184 electric sites)
- ❏ Deep Creek Lake (112 sites, 26 with electric)
- ❏ Elk Neck (200 sites, 50 with electric)
- ❏ Fort Frederick (29 primitive sites)
- ❏ Gambrill (34 sites, some with electric)
- ❏ Greenbrier (165 sites, 40 with electric)
- ❏ Janes Island (101 sites, many with electric)
- ❏ Martinak (63 sites, 30 with electric)
- ❏ New Germany (48 primitive sites)
- ❏ Patapsco Valley (26 electric sites)
- ❏ Pocomoke River (175 sites, some with electric)
- ❏ Point Lookout (143 sites, 26 full hookups and 33 electric only)
- ❏ Rocky Gap (278 sites, 30 with electric)
- ❏ Smallwood (15 electric sites)
- ❏ Susquehanna (69 sites, 6 with electric)

- Swallow Falls (65 water & electric)
- Tuckahoe (54 sites, 33 with electric)

MASSACHUSETTS

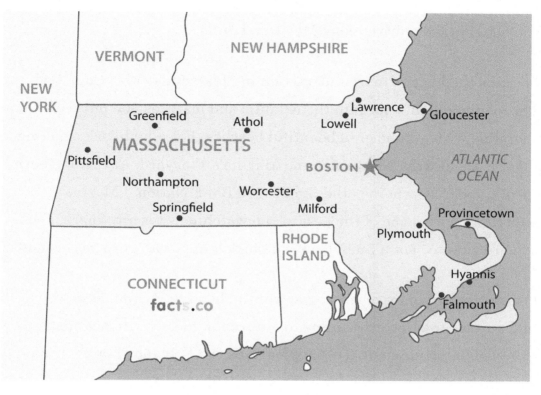

(Credit – www.Facts.co)

It is hard to find a simple description for Massachusetts. The state is rich in colonial history, has a strong art scene, features pristine beaches and offers some excellent culinary experiences. A popular destination within the state is Cape Cod with its beautiful shores, historic landmarks, rolling mountains and thick forests. Another popular destination is Boston full of galleries and museums.

Massachusetts features one of the biggest state park systems in the United States. Here you will find over 450,000 acres of beautiful landscapes, thick forests, and historic sites. In the west, hikers can enjoy the Appalachian Trail and Mt. Washington State Forest. Family picnic opportunities can be found at Royalston Falls and the Swift River Reservation. For a beautiful view of foliage when traveling in autumn, you should take a drive along Mohawk Trail.

Perhaps the biggest tourist attraction in Massachusetts is Cape Cod. This peninsula juts out into the Atlantic and features 560 miles of shoreline with a number of beautiful beaches. For a laid-back experience, there is the nearby Nantucket and Martha's Vineyard. At the northern tip of Cape Code, there is the Stellwagen Bank National Marine Sanctuary with some of the best whale watching sites anywhere. Here you are sure to spot a humpback whale, dolphin, seal, porpoise or more.

For a more urban experience, you want to head to Boston. Here you'll find a number of award-winning restaurants, historic attractions and plenty of entertainment. The city features the Freedom Trail, a three-mile path that takes you through some of the most famous national landmarks such as the USS Constitution, Old State House, and Faneuil Hall. For the art-inclined, you may want to stop by the Museum of Fine Arts, Isabella Stewart Gardner Museum and the Institute of Contemporary Art.

South of Boston you'll find the city of Plymouth, home to the first permanent European settlement in New England. You can visit the Plimoth Plantation, one of four living history museums in Massachusetts. This site is a 17th century English village that transports you back to Colonial America. In Plymouth Harbor, you can find a full-scale replica of the Mayflower while also learning about Native American history and culture. Nearby is the famous Pilgrim Memorial

State Park featuring the famous Plymouth Rock and Forefathers Monument.

However, there are plenty of other historical sites to visit in Massachusetts. Off Interstate 90 you'll find the town of Sturbridge featuring Old Sturbridge Village. Here you'll find over 40 antique buildings and historians in costume, so you have a chance to see what life was like in New England from 1790 to 1940.

In the town of Concord, you can visit Minuteman National Historic Park and the site of the opening battle of the American Revolution. Here you'll be able to tour preserved battlefields, fortifications and enough information to satisfy any history buff.

SUGGESTED MASSACHUSETTS RV TRIP

Massachusetts is known for its colonial history, and you'll see this no better than when you take the 84 mile trip from Sandwich to Salem in about two hours. There are plenty of things to see and do along the way to make this an enjoyable and long trip. Your trip begins in the small town of Sandwich that was settled in 1637. This small coastal town started as an industrial hub in the early days of New England. Stop by the Heritage Museum & Gardens to see a former plantation filled with blooming flowers. Or you can visit the Sandwich Glass Museum to see live glass blowing demonstrations and exhibits.

Heading north a short 19 miles, you'll reach the town of Plymouth in about 26 minutes. This is another town steeped in American history due to the 1620 landing at Plymouth Rock by the Pilgrim's. A must see is the

Plymouth Plantation; a living history museum featuring reenactments and interpreters for both colonial America as well as Native American.

Another short 40 minute trip of about 48 minutes takes you to the largest town on this trip, Boston. Boston served as the center of the American Revolution, and there are plenty of sites that allow you to relive this pivotal part of American History. See where it all began at the site of the Boston Tea Party in Boston Harbor and the street of the Boston Massacre.

Take the time to explore the Battle of Bunker Hill. Step aboard the USS Constitution, the oldest commissioned ship still sailing in the United States. There are also scores of other museums that you can see as you take a step back in time.

SUGGESTED RV PARKS

With so much to see and do while in Boston consider stopping at some of the excellent RV parks in the surrounding small towns. First is the Normandy Farms Family Camping Resort in the town of Foxboro. This park is pet-friendly with an enclosed dog run, a dog park and even pet boarding. There is a total of 365 sites open from April to November at the cost of $55 to $90. The park features the following amenities:

- ★ Internet
- ★ Restrooms and Showers
- ★ Laundry
- ★ ATM
- ★ RV Supplies
- ★ Metered LP Gas

- ★ Firewood
- ★ Ice
- ★ Snack Bar
- ★ Groceries
- ★ Onsite RV Service
- ★ Cable
- ★ Guest Services
- ★ Fishing Supplies
- ★ Heated Pool
- ★ Hot Tub
- ★ Fishing Pond
- ★ Horseshoes
- ★ Recreation Hall
- ★ Game Room
- ★ Playground
- ★ Outdoor Games
- ★ Pavilion
- ★ Sauna
- ★ Tennis
- ★ Shuffleboard
- ★ Exercise Room
- ★ Nature Trails
- ★ Frisbee Golf
- ★ Pickle Ball

Another option is the Circle CG Farm Campground in the town of Bellingham. This smaller park at 150 spaces is pet-friendly and open all year at the cost of $38 to $58 with the following amenities:

- ★ Internet
- ★ Restrooms and Showers
- ★ Laundry
- ★ RV Supplies
- ★ Metered LP Gas
- ★ Firewood
- ★ Ice
- ★ Groceries
- ★ Onsite RV Services
- ★ Cable
- ★ Guest Services
- ★ Swimming Pool
- ★ Fishing Pond
- ★ Horseshoes
- ★ Recreation Hall
- ★ Game Room
- ★ Outdoor Games
- ★ Pavilion
- ★ Tennis
- ★ Exercise Room
- ★ Nature Trails
- ★ Mini Golf
- ★ Pickle Ball

Lastly, consider the Boston Minuteman Campground in Littleton. This smaller site has 95 spaces and is only open from May to October at the cost of $49 to $61. The park is pet-friendly with the following amenities:

- ★ Internet

- ★ Restrooms and Showers
- ★ Laundry
- ★ RV Supplies
- ★ Metered LP Gas
- ★ Firewood
- ★ Ice
- ★ Groceries
- ★ Onsite RV Service
- ★ Cable
- ★ Guest Services
- ★ Heated Pool
- ★ Horseshoes
- ★ Recreation Hall
- ★ Game Room
- ★ Playground
- ★ Outdoor Games

The last leg of your trip covers about 25 miles and takes 32 minutes to reach Salem. This town is known for the witch trials in 1692. However, today it is one of the most visited town in Massachusetts. There is a number of historic sites to visit including the House of Seven Gables and the Witch House.

RV CAMPING AT MASSACHUSETTS STATE PARKS

AMENITIES

- Typical Cost: $12-$26
- Water: Almost Never (1 out of 23 parks)

- Electric: Rarely (3 out of 23 parks)
- Sewer: Never
- In/Out Rules: 14 night maximum, with some parks have a 2 night minimum.

MASSACHUSETTS STATE PARKS

- ❏ Erving State Forest (29 primitive sites)
- ❏ Lake Dennison Recreation Area (151 primitive sites)
- ❏ Otter River State Forest (78 primitive sites)
- ❏ Pearl Hill State Park (50 primitive sites)
- ❏ Wells State Park (60 sites)
- ❏ Harold Parker State Forest (91 primitive sites)
- ❏ Salisbury Beach State Reservation (484 water & electric)
- ❏ Willard Brook State Forest (21 primitive sites)
- ❏ Horseneck Beach State Reservation (100 primitive sites)
- ❏ Myles Standish State Forest (400 primitive sites)
- ❏ Nickerson State Park (403 primitive sites)
- ❏ Scusset Beach State Reservation (98 electric sites with shared water)
- ❏ Shawme-Crowell State Forest (285 primitive sites)
- ❏ Wompatuck State Park (450 sites, 140 with electric)
- ❏ Beartown State Forest (12 primitive sites)
- ❏ Clarksburg State Park (45 primitive sites)
- ❏ DAR State Forest (51 primitive sites)
- ❏ Granville State Forest (22 primitive sites)
- ❏ Mohawk Trail State Forest (47 primitive sites)
- ❏ October Mountain State Forest (44 primitive sites)
- ❏ Pittsfield State Forest (31 primitive sites)

- ❏ Savoy Mountain State Forest (45 primitive sites)
- ❏ Tolland State Forest (92 primitive sites)

MICHIGAN

The natural landscapes of Michigan range from blue waters to green grasslands; from sandy beaches to thick forests. The state is surrounded by four of the five Great Lakes and features some 12,000 inland lakes. The only state with more miles of coastline than Michigan is Alaska. However, you will find more lighthouses in the state of Michigan than anywhere else. There are plenty of outdoor places to explore in a state featuring over 100 state parks, forests and recreational areas.

The geography of Michigan is two peninsulas connected by the Mackinac Bridge, one of the longest suspension bridges in the world. The southern peninsula features several large cities such as Detroit. In the northern peninsula there are rural landscapes featuring stunning beauty. As you travel north, you will notice that the culture and dialects change to have more of a Canadian flair. The northern peninsula is home to most of the states 200 waterfalls.

Because of its many miles of coastline, Michigan has a number of protected shores. In the north, Pictured Rocks National Lakeshore is known for its unique rock formations within the sandstone cliffs of Lake Superior. Here you can take a hike on 90 miles of nature trails that showcase waterfalls, sand dunes, and wetlands. Another beautiful spot in the north is the Isle Royale National Park in the Porcupine Mountains region.

For an urban experience, Detroit is certainly a place to stop. Detroit has played a major role in defining American culture and industry. As the largest city in Michigan, Detroit has plenty of offer visitors. Multiple venues offer you arts and theater scenes such as the Detroit Institute of Arts or the Fox Theatre. Just outside of town in Dearborn, you'll find an indoor and outdoor museum complex for Henry Ford and the automotive history of the area.

For a break from everything consider a visit to Mackinac Island, located on Lake Huron. Cars are prohibited on this island, so you need to access it by a 16-minute ferry ride. Tour the island by horse-drawn carriage or cruiser bicycle. The centerpiece of the island is the Grand Hotel, which features one of the largest front porches in the world with beautiful views of the water.

SUGGESTED MICHIGAN RV TRIPS

Michigan is a vast and diverse state that requires two trips to see all that the great state has to offer. The first trip will take you a little off the beaten path to experience the beauty of the state on a short 67-mile trip that takes about an hour and a half. Start your trip enjoying the German culture in the small town of Frankenmuth. You'll find a variety of Bavarian culture and restaurants here to enjoy. Be sure to stop by the Holz Brucke bridge, the longest covered bridge in Michigan as it crosses the Cass River. It is a fine specimen of Bavarian craftsmanship.

SUGGESTED RV PARK

If you need a little extra time to explore all of the areas then consider staying at the Yogi Bear's Jellystone Park Camp-Resort. This 196 space, pet-friendly RV park is open from March to December at the cost of $48 to $79 with the following amenities:

- ★ Internet
- ★ Restrooms and Showers
- ★ Laundry
- ★ ATM
- ★ RV Supplies
- ★ Metered LP Gas
- ★ Firewood
- ★ Ice
- ★ Snack Bar
- ★ Groceries
- ★ Heated Pool

- ★ Hot Tub
- ★ Horseshoes
- ★ Recreation Hall
- ★ Game Room
- ★ Playground
- ★ Outdoor Games
- ★ Pavilion
- ★ Pedal Carts
- ★ Mini Golf

Your next destination is Bay City, about 21 miles and 30 minutes down the road. Bay City is located on the banks of the Saginaw River and is the perfect family-friendly destination. Both adults and kids will enjoy the Antique Toy and Fire Truck Museum. For the adults, you can enjoy relics at the Bay Antique Center. Or just head outdoors for a strong along the riverfront walk.

The last stop on this short trip is Mount Pleasant, about 46 miles and 56 minutes down the road. This town is home to the Central Michigan University and offers a variety of scenic landscapes. Visit the Ziibiwing Center to learn about Native American heritage; you'll see the culture and history of the Saginaw Chippewa Tribe as well as others.

SUGGESTED RV PARK AT MT. PLEASANT

While here consider staying a night at the Soaring Eagle Hideaway RV Park. This small, pet-friendly park only has 96 spaces. It is open from April to October at the cost of $35 to $74 with the following amenities:

- ★ Internet
- ★ Restrooms and Showers

- ★ Laundry
- ★ ATM
- ★ RV Supplies
- ★ Firewood
- ★ Snack Bar
- ★ Restaurant
- ★ Cocktail Lounge
- ★ Heated Pool
- ★ Boat Rentals
- ★ Hot Tub
- ★ Paddle Boats
- ★ Horseshoes
- ★ Recreation Hall
- ★ Game Room
- ★ Playground
- ★ Golf
- ★ Pavilion
- ★ Sauna
- ★ Nature Trails

Your second trip will take you along the western border of Michigan. This 178-mile trip will take you about three and a half hours to drive. The drive takes you through several of the quaint small towns of Michigan while enjoying the natural beauty of the state.

Start your trip out in the small town of Holland that truly makes you think you've traveled to the Netherlands. You'll find a number of Dutch-inspired attractions here including a tulip farm, a windmill, and a reproduction 19th-century Dutch village. You can also visit one of the most visited state parks in Michigan, Holland State Park with beautiful beaches along Lake Michigan.

The second stop on your trip is Silver Lake. It takes you about 72 miles and an hour and a half to get there. The draw here is the Silver Lake Sand Dunes with over 2,000 acres of sandy terrain. You can take part in a variety of outdoor activities from off-roading to sandboarding. In town, you can visit Little Sable Point Lighthouse in the nearby town of Mears and take the 130 steps to the top for some excellent views.

About an hour away, a short 53 miles is the town of Manistee. This town features a rich history matched only by the lush hiking trails in the surrounding area. There are 27 historic sites in downtown that will keep you occupied for the entire day. A must see is the Victorian antiques at the Manistee County Historical Museum. You can also take a historic trolley tour through the city, guided by people in period dress.

SUGGESTED RV PARK IN MANISTEE

With so much to see and do in this area, you may want to consider staying a few nights at the Insta Launch Campground and Marina. This 170 space park costs $37 and is open from April to November. Pets are welcome at this park that features the following amenities:

★ Internet
★ Restrooms and Showers
★ Laundry
★ RV Supplies
★ LP Bottles Only
★ Firewood

- ★ Ice
- ★ Snack Bar
- ★ Groceries
- ★ Self-Service RV Wash
- ★ Fishing Guides
- ★ Fishing Supplies
- ★ Boat Marina
- ★ Boat Rental
- ★ Horseshoes
- ★ Recreation Hall
- ★ Playground
- ★ Outdoor Games
- ★ Pavilion

The last stop on this trip is the Sleeping Bear Dunes National Lakeshore. It takes you about an hour to drive the 54 miles there. It is well worth the stop since it is considered one of the most scenic spots in all of the United States. You can enjoy a sandy shoreline with sweeping views of Lake Michigan. You should take a hike up to the viewpoint of Pyramid Point or walks around one of the many area museums to learn about the arts and culture.

RV CAMPING AT MICHIGAN STATE PARKS

AMENITIES

- Typical Cost: $12-$35
- Water: Rarely (6 out of 72 parks)
- Electric: Usually

- Sewer: Rarely (5 out of 72 parks)
- In/Out Rules: 15 night maximum.

MICHIGAN STATE PARKS

- ❑ Algonac (296 electric sites)
- ❑ Aloha (285 electric sites)
- ❑ Baraga (116 electric sites)
- ❑ Bay City (193 electric sites)
- ❑ Bewabic (144 electric sites)
- ❑ Big Bear Lake State Forest (11 primitive sites)
- ❑ Brighton Recreation Area (144 electric sites)
- ❑ Brimley (237 electric sites)
- ❑ Burt Lake (306 electric sites)
- ❑ Cheboygan (68 electric sites)
- ❑ Clear Lake (200 electric sites)
- ❑ Elk Hill (11 primitive sites)
- ❑ Fayette (61 electric sites)
- ❑ Fisherman's Island (80 primitive sites)
- ❑ Fort Custer Recreation Area (219 electric sites)
- ❑ Fort Wilkins Historic State Park (159 electric sites)
- ❑ Grand Haven (174 electric sites)
- ❑ Harrisville (195 electric sites)
- ❑ Hartwick Pines (100 full hookups)
- ❑ Hayes (185 electric sites)
- ❑ Highland Recreation Area (30 primitive sites)
- ❑ P.H. Hoeft (144 electric sites)
- ❑ P.J. Hoffmaster (293 electric sites)
- ❑ Holland (309 full hookups)

- ❏ Holly Recreation Area (144 electric sites)
- ❏ Indian Lake (200 electric sites)
- ❏ Interlochen (418 electric sites)
- ❏ Ionia Recreation Area (100 electric sites)
- ❏ Lake Gogebic (127 electric sites)
- ❏ Lake Hudson Recreation Area (50 electric sites)
- ❏ Lake Margrethe State Forest (37 primitive sites)
- ❏ Lakeport (251 water & electric)
- ❏ Leelanau (196 full hookups)
- ❏ Ludington (350 electric sites)
- ❏ F.J. McLain (104 electric sites)
- ❏ Charles Mears (175 electric sites)
- ❏ Metamora-Hadley State Recreation Area (214 electric sites)
- ❏ William Mitchell (221 electric sites)
- ❏ Muskallonge Lake (170 electric sites)
- ❏ Muskegon (244 electric sites)
- ❏ North Higgins Lake (174 electric sites)
- ❏ Onaway (97 electric sites and 200 full hookups)
- ❏ Orchard Beach (166 electric sites)
- ❏ Otsego Lake (155 electric sites)
- ❏ Petoskey (98 electric sites)
- ❏ Pinckney Recreation Area (186 electric sites)
- ❏ Pontiac Lake (176 electric sites)
- ❏ Porcupine Mountains (100 electric sites)
- ❏ Port Crescent (110 electric sites)
- ❏ Proud Lake Recreation Area (130 electric sites)
- ❏ Rifle River State Forest (180 electric sites)
- ❏ Seven Lakes (70 electric sites)
- ❏ Silver Lake (237 electric sites)

- ❏ Albert E. Sleeper (226 electric sites)
- ❏ Sleepy Hollow (181 electric sites)
- ❏ South Higgins Lake (400 electric sites)
- ❏ Sterling (256 full hookups)
- ❏ Straits (270 electric sites)
- ❏ Tahquamenon Falls (298 electric sites)
- ❏ Tawas Point (210 electric sites)
- ❏ Tippy Dam (41 primitive sites)
- ❏ Traverse City (480 electric sites)
- ❏ Twin Lakes (62 electric sites)
- ❏ Van Buren (220 electric sites)
- ❏ Van Riper (147 sites)
- ❏ Warren Dunes (100 electric sites)
- ❏ Waterloo Recreation Area (136 electric sites)
- ❏ J.W. Wells (178 electric sites)
- ❏ Wilderness (290 electric sites)
- ❏ Wilson (160 electric sites)
- ❏ Yankee Springs (200 electric sites and 12 primitive sites)
- ❏ Young (150 electric sites)

Minnesota is known as the Land of 10,000 lakes for a reason, the state is home to 11,842 lakes and features more shoreline than Hawaii, Florida, and California combined. This state is the premier destination for those who want to hike, boat, fish or take part in snow sports. However, there is plenty of urban luxuries in the Twin Cities of Minneapolis and St. Paul as well.

There are plenty of places in Minnesota to take advantage of water activities whether it be St. Croix River or Lake Superior. A state jewel is to visit Voyageurs National Park, which is only accessed by water. This

218,054-acre park features 30 lakes and offers a mix of history as well as natural beauty.

For more outdoor opportunities visit Superior National Forest in northeast Minnesota. One of the popular areas of this park is Boundary Waters Canoe Area Wilderness featuring 1,500 miles of canoe routes as well as over 1,000 lakes and streams. For fishers, there is an abundance of northern pike and smallmouth bass. Deep in the forest, there is also the International Wolf Center when you can watch a wolf pack and learn about these animals at the education center.

When it comes to an urban setting, the Twin Cities of Minneapolis and St. Paul offer plenty in the history, sports, art and culture department. The state capital of St. Paul features a number of historic buildings. Minneapolis is dedicated more to the upscale, contemporary crowd.

SUGGESTED MINNESOTA RV TRIP

Minnesota is a wonderful outdoor experience, and the best way to do this is to take a drive along the east coast of Minnesota. This 241-mile trip will take you about four hours and give you plenty of options for adventure. Start your trip in the small Mississippi River town of Wabasha. Here you'll find 50 Downtown buildings listed on the National Historic Register. Be sure to stop by the Wabasha's National Eagle Center so you can meet the majestic bald eagle. Along the mighty Mississippi, you can cruise in a sailboat, riverboat or kayak. There is no shortage of activities to keep you busy in this small town.

Continue your trip north to the urban center of Minneapolis. It is about 85 miles away and a trip of about two hours. Top on everyone's list when coming here is the 65,000 acre Paisley Park, home of music superstar Prince. You can also visit the Mall of America featuring over 520 stores, 50 restaurants, and an indoor theme park. At Minnehaha Park, you can hike to see a 50-foot waterfall.

Your next stop north is the town of Hinckley. It is another drive of about an hour and 81 miles. This small town is located between the two big urban hubs of Minneapolis and Duluth. Here you can visit the Grand Casino Hinckley with all sorts of gaming as well as dining and entertainment options. For the golfer, you can enjoy four golf courses with over ten miles of fairways. For the outdoor individual, you can't pass up kayaking down the Kettle or St. Croix River.

SUGGESTED RV PARKS

Since Hinckley is a middle ground between two big urban centers, it can be a good staging ground for your side trips. There are two recommended RV parks in this area that you can consider staying at while you explore everything in the surrounding area.

The first option is the Grand Casino Hinckley RV Resort. This 271 space RV park is pet-friendly and open all year. It costs $29 to $38 and features the following amenities:

★ Internet
★ Restrooms and Showers
★ Laundry
★ RV Supplies
★ Firewood
★ Ice

- ★ Snack Bar
- ★ Groceries
- ★ Restaurant
- ★ Cable
- ★ Guest Services
- ★ Self-Service RV Wash
- ★ Heated Pool
- ★ Horseshoes
- ★ Recreation Hall
- ★ Game Room
- ★ Playground
- ★ Outdoor Games
- ★ Driving Range
- ★ Pavilion
- ★ Sauna
- ★ Shuffleboard
- ★ Exercise Room

Another option is the St. Croix River Resort. This park offers 168 spaces open from May to October at a price of $55 to $59. It is a pet-friendly park with the following amenities:

- ★ Restrooms and Showers
- ★ Laundry
- ★ RV Supplies
- ★ Firewood
- ★ Ice
- ★ Groceries
- ★ Heated Pool

* ★ Boat Rentals
* ★ Horseshoes
* ★ Recreation Hall
* ★ Playground
* ★ Outdoor Games
* ★ Pavilion
* ★ Nature Trails
* ★ Bike Rentals

The last stop north in this trip is the second urban center of Duluth. This city is located on the banks of Lake Superior, the largest of the Great Lakes in the United States.

Visit Canal Park where you can sit on a bench and watch ships from around the world travel the Great Lakes. Take the time to watch the Aerial Lift Bridge raise and lower vertically. Learn the history of the waters in the area by visiting the Great Lakes Aquarium and the Maritime Visitor Center.

RV CAMPING AT MINNESOTA STATE PARKS

AMENITIES

* Typical Cost: $15-$31
* Water: No
* Electric: Almost Always
* Sewer: No
* In/Out Rules: 14 days maximum unless permission from a park ranger.

- ❏ Banning (33 sites, 11 electric)
- ❏ Bear Head Lake (73 sites, 45 electric)
- ❏ Beaver Creek Valley (42 sites, 16 electric)
- ❏ Big Bog State Recreation Area (31 sites, 26 electric)
- ❏ Big Stone Lake (37 sites, 10 electric)
- ❏ Blue Mounds (73 sites, 43 electric)
- ❏ Buffalo River (44 sites, 35 electric)
- ❏ Camden (80 sites, 29 electric)
- ❏ Carley (20 primitive sites)
- ❏ Cascade River (38 sites, 15 electric, 40 primitive sites)
- ❏ Crow Wing (59 sites, 12 electric)
- ❏ Cuyuna Country State Recreation Area (25 primitive sites)
- ❏ Father Hennepin (103 sites, 51 electric)
- ❏ Flandrau (92 sites, 34 electric)
- ❏ Forestville/Mystery Cave (73 sites, 23 electric)
- ❏ Fort Ridgely (31 sites, 15 electric)
- ❏ Franz Jevne (18 sites, 1 electric)
- ❏ Frontenac (58 sites, 19 electric)
- ❏ Glacial Lakes (37 sites, 14 electric)
- ❏ Gooseberry Falls (69 primitive sites)
- ❏ Great River Bluffs (31 primitive sites)
- ❏ Hayes Lakes (35 sites, 18 electric)
- ❏ Interstate (37 sites, 22 electric)
- ❏ Itasca (223 sites, 160 electric)
- ❏ Jay Cooke (79 sites, 21 electric)
- ❏ Judge C.R. Magney (27 primitive sites)
- ❏ Kilen Woods (33 sites, 11 electric)

- ❏ La Salle Lake State Recreation Area (39 electric)
- ❏ Lac Qui Parle (77 sites, 58 electric)
- ❏ Lake Bemidji (95 sites, 43 electric)
- ❏ Lake Bronson (152 sites, 67 electric)
- ❏ Lake Carlos (121 sites, 81 electric)
- ❏ Lake Louise (20 sites, 11 electric)
- ❏ Lake Shetek (70 sites, 64 electric)
- ❏ McCarthy Beach (86 sites, 21 electric)
- ❏ Maplewood (71 sites, 32 electric)
- ❏ Mille Lacs Kathio (70 sites, 22 electric)
- ❏ Minneopa (61 sites, 6 electric)
- ❏ Monson Lake (20 primitive sites)
- ❏ Myre - Big Island (93 sites, 32 electric)
- ❏ Nerstrand Big Woods (51 sites, 27 electric)
- ❏ Old Mill (26 sites, 10 electric)
- ❏ Red River State Recreation Area (109 sites, 85 electric)
- ❏ Rice Lake (40 sites, 18 electric)
- ❏ St. Croix (211 sites, 81 electric)
- ❏ Sakatah Lake (62 sites, 14 electric)
- ❏ Savanna Portage (61 sites, 18 electric)
- ❏ Scenic (93 sites, 23 electric)
- ❏ Schoolcraft (28 primitive sites)
- ❏ Sibley (132 sites, 53 electric)
- ❏ Split Rock Creek (34 sites, 21 electric)
- ❏ Temperance River (52 sites, 18 electric)
- ❏ Tettegouche (28 sites, 22 electric)
- ❏ Upper Sioux Agency (34 sites, 14 electric)
- ❏ Whitewater (104 sites, 47 electric)
- ❏ Wild River (94 sites, 34 electric)

❏ William O'Brien (112 sites, 70 electric)

❏ Zippel Bay (57 primitive sites)

(Credit – www.Facts.co)

Mississippi is a complex state; it is the birthplace of blues music, was a pivotal point in many Civil War battles and is a state full of natural beauty. There is plenty to see and do in this state.

Mississippi is a popular destination for outdoor lovers since it features year-round warm weather, a lot of wildlife viewing and stunning natural beauty. The best way to see all of this is by the Natchez Trace Parkway. This highway covers 444 miles from Natchez to Nashville and was once a historic route used by the Native Americans and later the pioneering settlers. While driving this route you are likely to spot waterfowl, deer, armadillo, wild turkey and more. You can stop along the way to walk interpretive trails or other sites.

If you want to visit urban settings, then look no further than the state capital of Jackson. Here you'll find a range of music, culture, and history to explore. Some of the top attractions in this city include the Old Capitol Museum, Museum of Natural Science, Jackson Zoological Park and the Mississippi Museum of Art. If history is more your thing, then stop by Vicksburg to see the National Military Park, one of the sites of the most important Civil War battles in 1863.

SUGGESTED MISSISSIPPI RV TRIP

Mississippi is a state with big water, whether it be the Gulf Coast or the Mississippi River. The best RV trip in the state takes you on a journey between these two waters to see the best that the state has to offer. The trip will cover 301 miles and take you about five hours to drive.

Start your trip on the Mississippi Sound in the town of Biloxi, known for its entertainment. You can choose to game at the local casinos or walk around the historic district of Biloxi. Head to the beaches to take in the sun or get out on the water for some water activities.

Suggested RV Park

In Biloxi, you can choose to stay at the Cajun RV Park. This park is open all year with 130 spaces at the cost of $42 to $63. This pet-friendly park features the following amenities:

- ★ Internet
- ★ Restrooms and Showers
- ★ Laundry
- ★ RV Supplies
- ★ Metered LP Gas
- ★ Ice
- ★ Cable
- ★ Complimentary Breakfast
- ★ Guest Services
- ★ Self-Service RV Wash
- ★ Swimming Pool
- ★ Horseshoes
- ★ Recreation Hall
- ★ Playground
- ★ Outdoor Games
- ★ Pavilion

Laurel is your second stop after a drive of 109 miles that takes about two hours. Walking the town's historic district will take you back in time. The town is listed on the National Register of Historic Places and features some of the biggest and best maintained 20th-century architecture in Mississippi. Take the time to visit the Lauren Rogers Museum of Art to see exhibits on American, European and Japanese art.

Next stop, Jackson. 89 miles and about an hour and a half drive. Jackson is the capital of Mississippi and allows you to see the combination of the past and present. Walk down the Mississippi Freedom Trail to learn about Civil Rights leaders and events.

The last stop on this trip is Natchez. It is 103 miles down the road and trip of about two hours. This historic small town is the gateway to the Mississippi River. You must visit the famous Dunleith Plantation to view buildings dating back to the 1790s. Take the time to bike or hike a portion of the 444 miles long Natchez Trace Parkway that covers 10,000 years of American history.

RV CAMPING AT MISSISSIPPI STATE PARKS

AMENITIES

- Typical Cost: $13-$30
- Water: Yes
- Electric: Yes
- Sewer: Usually

MISSISSIPPI STATE PARKS

- ❏ Buccaneer (301 full hookups)
- ❏ Clarkco (79 full hookups)
- ❏ George P. Cossar (30 full hookups)
- ❏ Golden Memorial (16 water & electric)
- ❏ Holmes County (28 water & electric)
- ❏ Hugh White (30 water & electric)

- ❏ John W. Kyle (220 full hookups)
- ❏ J.P. Coleman (69 full hookups)
- ❏ Lake Lincoln (86 full hookups)
- ❏ Lake Lowndes (58 full hookups)
- ❏ Legion (34 full hookups)
- ❏ Leroy Percy (24 full hookups)
- ❏ Natchez (68 water & electric)
- ❏ Paul B. Johnson (155 full hookups)
- ❏ Percy Quin (180 full hookups)
- ❏ Roosevelt (124 full hookups)
- ❏ Shepard (28 water & electric)
- ❏ Tishomingo (69 water & electric)
- ❏ Tombigbee (37 full hookups)
- ❏ Trace (70 full hookups)
- ❏ Wall Doxey (91 water & electric)

Missouri is known as the land of adventure. St. Louis is the spot where Lewis and Clark started their Corps of Discovery Expedition in 1804. As more pioneers and adventurers followed, St. Louis became known as the Gateway to the West.

Missouri is truly a Midwestern state in its landscape, sense of adventure and hospitality. The terrain in this state varies from rolling hills in the northern plains to the majestic and towering Ozark Mountains in the south. The state boasts three thriving cities in St. Louis, Kansas City, and Springfield.

It is no wonder you can have plenty of outdoor adventures in Missouri since it is full of mountains, bluffs, springs, forests and even underground caves. Missouri has been nicknamed the Cave State and features over 5,000 caves. Your best option for this is the Elephant Rocks State Park, where you will see 1.5 billion-year-old granite boulders at the 129-acre park.

If hiking is more your thing, then consider the Ozark Trail. This 550-mile long trail is a counterpart to the Appalachian Trail. Hiking this trail will take you through forests and creeks while taking you to the summit of two mountains: Stegall Mountain and Taum Sauk Mountain.

St. Louis has grown into a cosmopolitan city from its roots as a trading post, but still maintains several landmarks and museums that showcase the city's rich history. Perhaps the biggest landmark is the 630-foot high Gateway Arch that celebrates Thomas Jefferson's vision of expanding westward. You can take a tram ride to the top of the arch, or you can visit the Museum of Westward Expansion to learn about the expansion of the United States following the Louisiana Purchase.

Kansas City is another spot to hit if you are into urban exploration. Here you can visit the National World War I Museum which is the second largest of its kind in the entire world. This city is also home to the American Jazz Museum. Another city you can visit is Springfield which was the birthplace of the first telegraph line and features a stretch of the famous Route 66.

If you are RV traveling with a family, then you may want to consider a stop in Branson. Here you can enjoy a variety of live entertainment, mini-golf, wax museums and several theme parks.

SUGGESTED MISSOURI RV TRIP

Missouri is a state of beautiful outdoor activities as well as urban fun. The trip of choice takes you about 259 miles in 4 hours of driving time. During the trip you'll get to travel from the major urban centers Branson to St. Louis while exploring some beautiful outdoor options along the way.

Start your trip in the urban center of St. Louis. This was the historic gateway for many settlers heading west in the 1800s; this is now memorialized by the 630-foot tall Gateway Arch. St. Louis is a wonderful city with lots of free activities to enjoy. First, you want to stop by the Missouri History Museum; there is plenty of subjects to learn about at this museum that will keep you busy for hours. If you have children, you'll want to stop by the St. Louis Science Center for a lot of hands-on fun. The St. Louis Art Museum is also free, plus it has a kids section so it is an art museum that can be enjoyed by the whole family.

St. Louis is also home to one of the few free zoos still in the United States. This is a large zoo that will likely take you a whole day to walk around and see. If you enjoy animals, you'll also want to consider taking a trip to Purina Farms. Here you can watch dogs train, visit the cat's tree house and see a working farm. Another option is Grant's Farm where you can view Clydesdales, elephants and more. Feed goats, explore deer park and watch a range of animal shows at this farm. Lastly, visit the World Bird Sanctuary.

Once you have finished seeing all there is to do in the city; you are ready for an outdoor adventure by heading to Meramec Caverns. This is a trip of about 64 miles and takes about an hour to drive. This is one of the most popular tourist destinations along Route 66. Meramec Caverns is 400 million years old and spaces 4.5 miles. The caves are made from natural limestone and have been used as a shelter for Native Americans to Civil War soldiers.

Your next outdoor experience is 68 miles down the road, about an hour drive at Devils Elbow. This is the name of the sharp turn in the Big Piney River that resulted in many logjams for timber rafters that worked in the area. Stop to hike the many trails in this historic area of Route 66. Be sure to stop for some authentic Missouri barbeque at the Elbow Inn bar.

End your trip at another urban destination, Branson. It is about a two-hour drive and 127 miles down the road. When it comes to entertainment in the Midwest, Branson is the capital. There are a range of theaters in this town that has put on many top entertainers. You can also visit the Silver Dollar City, an amusement park with a range of attractions. For an outdoor adventure, you can visit nearby Table Rock Lake and Marvel Cave Park.

SUGGESTED RV PARK

If you need some extra time to explore the area around Branson, then consider staying at America's Best Campground. This 160 space RV park is open year-round at the cost of $44. It is pet-friendly and features the following amenities:

* ★ Internet
* ★ Restrooms and Showers
* ★ Laundry
* ★ RV Supplies
* ★ Metered LP Gas
* ★ Ice
* ★ Groceries
* ★ Guest Services
* ★ Self-Service RV Wash
* ★ Swimming Pool
* ★ Hot Tub
* ★ Horseshoes
* ★ Recreation Hall
* ★ Playground
* ★ Outdoor Games
* ★ Pavilion

RV CAMPING AT MISSOURI STATE PARKS

AMENITIES

* Typical Cost: $10-$56
* Water: Often (19 out of 39 parks)
* Electric: Yes
* Sewer: Sometimes (16 parks have full hookups)
* In/Out Rules: 15 night maximum in a 30 day period.

MISSOURI STATE PARKS

- ❏ Arrow Rock State Historic Sites (full hookups)
- ❏ Dr. Edmund A. Babler Memorial State Park
- ❏ Sam A. Baker State Park
- ❏ Battle of Athens State Historic Park
- ❏ Bennett Spring State Park (full hookups available)
- ❏ Big Lake State Park
- ❏ Crowder State Park
- ❏ Cuivre River State Park (full hookups available)
- ❏ Finger Lakes State Park
- ❏ Graham Cave State Park
- ❏ Hawn State Park
- ❏ Johnson's Shut-Ins State Park (full hookups available)
- ❏ Knob Noster State Park
- ❏ Lake Wappapello
- ❏ Lake of the Ozarks State Park
- ❏ Lewis and Clark State Park
- ❏ Long Branch
- ❏ Meramec State Park (full hookups available)
- ❏ Montauk State Park
- ❏ Onondaga Cave State Park
- ❏ Pershing State Park
- ❏ Pomme de Terre State Park
- ❏ Prairie State Park
- ❏ Roaring River State Park (full hookups available with premium campsites)
- ❏ Robertsville State Park
- ❏ St. Francois State Park

- ❏ St. Joe State Park
- ❏ Stockton State Park
- ❏ Table Rock State Park (full hookups available)
- ❏ Taum Sauk Mountain State Park
- ❏ Thousand Hills State Park
- ❏ Trail of Tears State Park (full hookups available)
- ❏ Harry S. Truman State Park
- ❏ Mark Twain State Park
- ❏ Van Meter State Park
- ❏ Wakonda State Park (full hookups available)
- ❏ Wallace State Park
- ❏ Washington State Park
- ❏ Weston Bend State Park

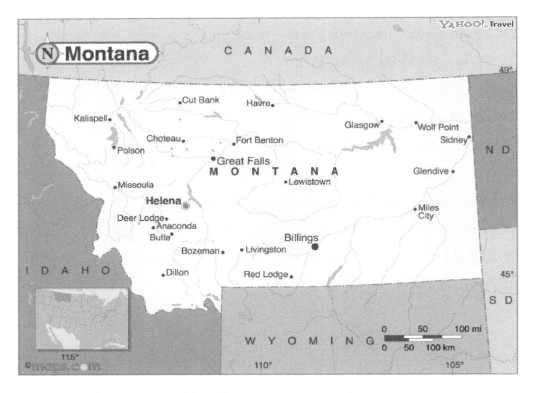

(Credit – www.Maps.com)

While Montana is the fourth largest state in the US, it is one of the least populated. This means you have plenty of outdoor space to explore in a geographic area that ranges from vast plains to the rugged Rocky Mountains.

You can view a number of iconic natural attractions in Montana. Near the Canadian border, you want to visit Glacier National Park. It features over 700 miles of hiking and biking trails through a wide range of landscapes. You can view mountain goats, bighorn sheep and over 260 species of birds.

A little farther south you'll find the Lewis and Clark Caverns, State Park. Here you can explore limestone caverns underground, or you can hike above ground on over 10 miles of hiking trails.

Perhaps the best-known park in Montana is Yellowstone National Park; the first national park in the United States. Known for its powerful geysers and hot springs, the park also features beautiful lakes, forests, and mountains. You can also visit the Grizzly and Wolf Discovery Center to have an opportunity to see these magnificent creatures.

There are also a number of vibrant towns to visit in Montana despite the low population. Bozeman offers a unique city experience with festivals, farmers markets, theaters and art galleries. The city is home to the Museum of the Rockies which is known for the largest dinosaur collection in the United States.

SUGGESTED MONTANA RV TRIP

Montana is a state of wide open wilderness space. Take an RV trip that takes you from the city of Missoula up to the breathtaking natural beauty of Glacier National Park. The trip is 219 miles and will take you about four hours to drive, but with plenty to keep you busy for days.

Start your trip in the city of Missoula, also a beautiful location nestled within five peaks of the Rocky Mountains. From anywhere you'll be able to catch a glimpse of the local wildlife including deer, bear, osprey, bald eagles and plenty more. There is plenty of outdoor activities including kayaking, trout fishing and walking. There is also plenty of urban options, including a few breweries to enjoy.

Continue your trip about an hour down the road to the town of Polson in about 70 miles. This is a city of contrasts: on one side you can enjoy free public beaches at this lakeside town, but you can also have easy access to snow-peaked Mission Mountains. The agriculture valley makes it ideal for bird watching as well as the National Bison Range. In town, you can enjoy a live theater, museums, and galleries; all with a small town charm.

After a 116 mile trip of about two hours, you'll come to the town of Kalispell. Along the way, you'll pass Flathead Lake and the heart of the Rocky Mountains as you get closer to nature. This town is the largest city in northwest Montana and is the gateway to the Glacier National Park. The town also has deep frontier roots that you can see everywhere, but particularly in historic downtown.

End your trip with a short 45-minute drive to cover the 33 miles to Glacier National Park and the peak of natural beauty. This spectacular park is over one million square miles and encompasses the US/Canadian border. Waters from this park actually make their way to Hudson Bay, the Gulf of Mexico and even the Pacific Ocean. You'll get the chance to see wildlife such as bears, moose, mountain goats, wolverines, and lynxes. There is plenty of wonderful hiking and driving opportunities in this park.

RV CAMPING AT MONTANA STATE PARKS

AMENITIES

- Typical Cost: $24-$34
- Water: Sometimes

- Electric: Often
- Sewer: No

MONTANA STATE PARKS

- ❏ Ackley Lake (15 sites)
- ❏ Bannack (28 sites)
- ❏ Beavertail Hill (28 sites)
- ❏ Big Arm (70 sites, 44 electric)
- ❏ Black Sandy (29 sites)
- ❏ Brush Lake
- ❏ Cooney (72 sites, 13 electric)
- ❏ Finley Point (16 water & electric)
- ❏ Hell Creek (55 sites, 45 electric)
- ❏ Lake Mary Ronan (25 electric sites)
- ❏ Lewis & Clark Caverns (40 sites)
- ❏ Logan (37 sites)
- ❏ Lost Creek (25 sites)
- ❏ Medicine Rocks (12 sites)
- ❏ Makoshika (16 sites)
- ❏ Missouri Headwaters (17 sites)
- ❏ Painted Rocks (25 sites)
- ❏ Placid Lake (40 sites)
- ❏ Salmon Lake (20 sites)
- ❏ Thompson Falls (17 sites)
- ❏ Tongue River Reservoir (150 sites, 40 electric)
- ❏ Wayfarers (40 sites)
- ❏ West Shore (24 sites)
- ❏ Whitefish Lake (25 sites)

(Credit – www.theodora.com/maps)

If you take an RV trip to Nebraska, you'll quickly discover why the state is called the Great Plains region. While it may seem like endless expanses of green fields, there are beautiful pine forests and sand hills in the western part of the state. There are also a few cities to the east ready to welcome you on your adventure.

When it comes to an outdoor experience, you should consider Smith Falls State Park; which includes the state's largest waterfall. Other outdoor options are a hike along the Cowboy Recreation and Nature Trail.

After all the open land of the Great Plains, you may not expect to see the towering skyscrapers of Omaha along the eastern border. While here you should visit the Henry Doorly Zoo and Aquarium which offers a sky tram to take you above the animals as well as a geodesic dome that features a desert habitat.

SUGGESTED NEBRASKA RV TRIP

There is one RV trip that allows you to see the best Nebraska has to offer. It is a 186-mile trip that takes you through Omaha, Lincoln, and Kearney in a drive of about three hours with plenty of activities to last days.

Your trip starts in the biggest city in Nebraska, Omaha. The best place to start is just south of town at Fontenelle Forest. This area has over 26 miles of maintained trails that are great for hiking the outdoors. In town, be sure to visit the Durham Museum located at the 1930s art deco union station. You'll also want to take a walk across the Bob Kerrey Pedestrian Bridge. This 3,000-foot long suspension bridge will give you an airborne experience as you cross the longest pedestrian bridge to link two states.

It also serves to connect over 150 miles of walking and hiking trails. Also consider a walk through the 31 acres Heartland of America Park with a 300-foot water and light show in the fountain, or you can take a gondola ride around the park. Lastly, for a unique art experience take the First National's Spirit of Nebraska's Wilderness and Pioneer Courage Park walk. This consists of over 100 individual bronze pieces in size from 400 pounds to six tons that tell the story of a stampede of buffalo through buildings.

Your second stop is Lincoln, about 53 miles down the road. It takes about 58 minutes to get to the capital of Nebraska. In this city, there are plenty of interesting historical sites to visit. Plus there is a range of educational sites to visit: Sheldon Museum of Art, University of Nebraska State Museum, International Quilt Study Center & Museum and more.

You'll also want to spend some time outdoors such as Pioneer Park Nature Center with 668 acres to enjoy. Lastly, be sure to stop by the Lincoln Children's Zoo with a train ride if you come between April and October.

End your trip 133 miles down the road in Kearny after a two-hour drive. At first, this may seem like a small town, but it actually has a lot to offer; especially when you visit the Archway Museum. This is both a monument to the United States expansion west as well as a repository for historical artifacts. You can even rent a paddle boat to tour around the city for a unique perspective.

RV CAMPING AT NEBRASKA STATE PARKS

AMENITIES

- Typical Cost: $8-$26
- Water: Often
- Electric: Often
- Sewer: Often
- In/Out Rules: 14 days maximum, except in extended stay areas.

NEBRASKA STATE PARKS

The following start parks offer modern RV camping:

- ❏ Branched Oak State Recreation Area
- ❏ Calamus State Recreation Area
- ❏ Enders State Recreation Area
- ❏ Fort Kearney State Recreation Area
- ❏ Fremont State Recreation Area
- ❏ Indian Cave State Park
- ❏ Johnson Lake State Recreation Area
- ❏ Lake McConaughy State Recreation Area
- ❏ Lake Minatare State Recreation Area
- ❏ Lake Ogallala State Recreation Area
- ❏ Lake Wanahoo State Recreation Area
- ❏ Louisville State Recreation Area
- ❏ Medicine Creek State Recreation Area
- ❏ Mormon Island State Recreation Area
- ❏ Pawnee Lake State Recreation Area
- ❏ Red Willow State Recreation Area
- ❏ Rock Creek Station State Historical Park
- ❏ Smith Falls State Park
- ❏ Swanson Lake State Recreation Area
- ❏ Willow Creek State Recreation Area
- ❏ Windmill State Recreation Area

PRIMITIVE CAMPING SITES IN STATE PARKS

The following state parks offer primitive camping only:

- ❏ Alexandria State Recreation Area (46 electric sites)
- ❏ Bluestem State Recreation Area (219 sites)
- ❏ Box Butte Reservoir State Recreation Area (54 sites, 14 electric)

- Bridgeport State Recreation Area (130 sites)
- Buffalo Bill Ranch State Recreation Area (29 sites, 23 electric)
- Cheyenne State Recreation Area (8 sites)
- Conestoga State Recreation Area (57 sites, 25 electric)
- Cottonwood Lake State Recreation Area (30 sites)
- Dead Timber State Recreation Area (42 sites, 17 electric)
- Gallagher Canyon State Recreation Area (25 sites)
- Keller Park State Recreation Area (35 sites, 25 electric)
- Lake Maloney State Recreation Area (256 sites, 56 electric)
- Long Pine State Recreation Area (28 sites)
- Memphis State Recreation Area (150 sites)
- Merritt Reservoir State Recreation Area (218 sites, 28 electric)
- Olive Creek State Recreation Area (50 sites)
- Oliver Reservoir State Recreation Area (175 sites)
- Pibel Lake State Recreation Area (30 sites)
- Riverview Marina State Recreation Area (46 sites, 16 electric)
- Rockford State Recreation Area (107 sites, 30 electric)
- Sherman Reservoir State Recreation Area (360 sites)
- Stagecoach State Recreation Area (72 sites, 22 electric)
- Summit Lake State Recreation Area (67 sites, 30 electric)
- Sutherland Reservoir State Recreation Area (85 sites)
- Union Pacific State Recreation Area (5 sites)
- Verdon State Recreation Area (20 sites)
- Wagon Train State Recreation Area (108 sites, 28 electric)
- Walgren Lake State Recreation Area (40 sites)
- War Axe State Recreation Area (8 sites)

❑ Wildcat Hills State Recreation Area (5 sites)

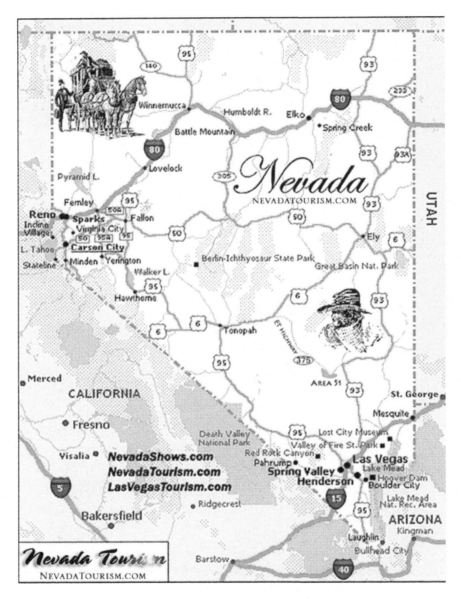

(Credit – www.NevadaTourism.com)

Nevada is a state of contrasts: it is home to the Loneliest Road in America along the stretch of US Route 50, and on the other hand, it is home to one of the most visited cities in the United States, Las Vegas. In between these contrasts you'll find a diverse range of landscapes from arid red rocks in the south to sparkling blue waters in the north. There is plenty that Nevada has to offer.

Anyone visiting Nevada obviously starts their trip in Las Vegas. In this city, you can visit a number of gaming casinos and theaters. However, there is still plenty of other attractions in the state for those who would rather have an outdoor adventure.

Just outside of Las Vegas there is the Red Rock Canyon National Conservation Area and a little farther away is the Valley of Fire State Park. Nearly the border with Utah you'll find the Great Basin National Park which offers you a scenic change from the desert landscape with lush blue and green landscapes. You'll even find snow-covered mountain peaks with pine trees.

A popular Nevada destination near Las Vegas is Lake Mead. This lake is created at the point where the Hoover Dam blocks the Colorado River and forms one of the largest reservoirs in the United States. Another popular body of water is Lake Tahoe, which straddles the border with California. Both of these locations offer plenty of fishing, boating and hiking options.

SUGGESTED NEVADA RV TRIP

Nevada is a known stop for those who want to head to the gambling casinos of Las Vegas or catch an entertainment show at one of the many casinos. However, there is plenty of other things to see and do in this state. Take the suggested RV trip of 124 miles from Las Vegas to

Laughlin so you can see everything this state has to offer in about two hours driving time.

Start your trip in what is known as the best gambling destination in the world, Las Vegas. Here you can gamble, watch live shows or enjoy excellent food. But there is more to this city and plenty of free attractions to enjoy as well. Plenty of the casinos and resorts have free entertainment right out front. Every evening you can watch a pirate ship battle on Buccaneer Bay. The Mirage has the Volcano Fountain since 1989 with a three-acre water display that is 54 feet high and circulates 119,000 gallons of water a minute. The Bellagio also has a fountain show that includes water, music, and light.

There are also a few other worthwhile free things to check out while in Las Vegas. Be sure to check out the MGM Grand Lion Habitat where you can see retired lions on an 8.5 acres ranch 12 miles from the MGM Grand hotel. Another option is the Bellagio Botanical Conservatory where you can enjoy natural finds from throughout the world. Lastly, there is the Mirage Aquarium. It is a 20,000-gallon saltwater aquarium with angelfish, puffer fish, tangs, sharks and other exotic fish.

The aquarium also has over 1,000 coral reef animals from 60 species in Australia, Hawaii, Tonga, Fiji, the Red Sea, the Marshall Islands, the Sea of Cortez and the Caribbean. This is known as one of the most elaborate and technically advanced aquariums in the world at 53 feet long, 8 feet tall and 6 feet wide.

After you've tired of the city, take a drive of just 33 minutes or 26 miles to the town of Boulder City for a different experience. This is one of the few spots in the state where gambling is prohibited. However, the draw here is the Hoover Dam and its museum along with Lake Mead, the largest reservoir in the United States.

SUGGESTED RV PARK

Since Boulder City is the middle destination in this RV road trip, it can make for a great staging area if you want to stay at the Lake Mead RV Village. This 115 space RV park is pet-friendly and open year round at a rate of $30 to $45 with the following amenities:

- ★ Internet
- ★ Restrooms and Showers
- ★ Laundry
- ★ RV Supplies
- ★ Metered LP Gas
- ★ Firewood
- ★ Ice
- ★ Groceries
- ★ Cable
- ★ Horseshoes
- ★ Recreation Hall
- ★ Exercise Room
- ★ Nature Trails

Laughlin is the last stop on your RV trip. It is about 97 miles and an hour and a half from Boulder City. This town is considered the quieter version of Las Vegas or Reno but still offers plenty in the way of casinos, entertainment and a number of other activities for those who want a little less urban appeal. Since the town is located on the Colorado River, you can easily take part in water sports such as skiing, boating, swimming, and fishing.

RV CAMPING AT NEVADA STATE PARKS

AMENITIES

- Typical Cost: $21-$30
- Water: Rarely (1 out of 15 parks)
- Electric: Rarely (2 out of 15 parks)
- Sewer: Rarely (1 out of 15 parks)
- In/Out Rules: 14 days in a 30 day period.

NEVADA STATE PARKS

- ❑ Beaver Dam State Park (69 sites)
- ❑ Berlin-Ichthyosaur (14 sites)
- ❑ Big Bend of Colorado (24 full hookups)
- ❑ Cathedral Gorge (22 electric sites)
- ❑ Cave Lake (75 sites)
- ❑ Echo Canyon (33 sites)
- ❑ Fort Churchill State Historic Park (20 sites)
- ❑ Kershaw-Ryan (15 sites)
- ❑ Rye Patch State Recreation Area (47 sites)
- ❑ South Fork State Recreation Area (25 sites)
- ❑ Spring Valley (37 sites)
- ❑ Valley of Fire (72 sites)
- ❑ Ward Charcoal
- ❑ Washoe Lake (49 sites)
- ❑ Wild Horse State Recreation Area (33 sites)

New Hampshire offers you everything you would expect of a New England state; complete with natural beauty, small towns, and historic farms and orchards. While this state only has 18 miles of coastline, it still features a strong English fishing history that dates back to the 1600s. If you want to get a feel for colonial history then you should head to Portsmouth and Dover.

Fo an outdoor experience you want to head to the White Mountains that dominate the skyline to the north. You can drive this range along the Kancamagus Highway which offers a number of scenic stops with breathtaking views. Along this drive, you should stop to see Sabbaday Falls and its stunning 45-foot drop.

Another option is the Rocky Gorge, which features a footbridge over the Swift River. You can also summit Mount Washington, the tallest peak in the state. A unique experience is to take the historic cog railway to the top.

At the northeast border of the state near Maine, you'll find the seaport of Portsmouth. Here you'll feel as if you've stepped back in time. From Prescott Park, you can take a break and watch the ships sailing along Piscataqua River. Or you can take a stroll through the outdoor Strawbery Banke Museum which is 10 acres of restored buildings dating back to the 1600s.

SUGGESTED NEW HAMPSHIRE RV TRIP

New Hampshire is a small and rugged state with a five-city road trip that shows you all the state has to offer. You can cover these five cities within about 88 miles and two hours driving time, with lots of time to spend doing activities. Start your trip in the town of Campton, originally a 1700s surveyor's camp.

Here you can check out a historic home, a beautiful waterfall, a boat tour and plenty of other activities. However, a must-see is the 1869 Blair Bridge, a covered bridge that spans nearly 300 feet across the Pemigewasset River; nearly the size of a football field.

A short 24-minute drive of 20 miles will take you to the second city on the trip, Lincoln. Here you are sure to find an outdoor activity, no matter what your interest. If you want to have a different experience, take the Hobo Railroad for a 15-mile ride in the countryside. For kids, you should stop by the Whale's Tale water park. Or another way to see the area is to take Lincoln's Summer Safari Tours in a six-wheeling outdoor adventure. Others travel options include skiing, biking, hiking and even horseback riding.

It is another short 30-minute drive of 24 miles to the third town of Carroll. Here you need to take a ride on the Mt. Washington Cog Railway. This three-hour trip is gravity defying as you travel up the tallest mountain in New England. You can even choose to ride an old-fashioned steam engine train or a modern eco-conscious biodiesel-powered train.

The fourth town on the trip is another short 40 minutes or 31 miles down the road, Glen. While the rugged mountains are breathtaking, the draw here is Story Land theme park. Here you'll find over 35 acres of attractions, rides and family fun; including an antique German Carousel

Lastly, end your trip in the town of Conway. It is another short trip of 23 minutes to drive 13 miles. Here you can take a step back in time with the Conway Scenic Railroad. You will be able to take a vintage passenger car ride along historic routes while enjoying mountain vistas. You can even take part in themed train rides.

RV CAMPING AT NEW HAMPSHIRE STATE PARKS

AMENITIES

- Typical Cost: $23-$50
- Water: Rarely (3 out of 18 parks)
- Electric: Rarely (3 out of 18 parks)
- Sewer: Rarely (2 out of 18 parks)
- In/Out Rules: 14 days maximum. If reserving before April 1st there is a 3 night minimum.

NEW HAMPSHIRE STATE PARKS

- ❏ Bear Brook (101 primitive sites)
- ❏ Coleman (25 primitive sites)
- ❏ Crawford Notch (36 primitive sites)
- ❏ Connecticut Lakes (25 primitive sites)
- ❏ Ellacoya (47 full hookups)
- ❏ Franconia Notch (7 full hookups)
- ❏ Greenfield (45 primitive sites)
- ❏ Hampton Beach (28 full hookups)
- ❏ Lake Francis (45 sites)
- ❏ Milan Hill
- ❏ Mollidgewock (42 primitive sites)
- ❏ Monadnock (primitive sites)
- ❏ Moose Brook (59 sites)

- Mount Sunapee (primitive sites)
- Pawtuckaway (192 primitive sites)
- Pillsbury (primitive sites)
- Umbagog Lake (27 water & electric)
- White Lake (primitive sites)

New Jersey is one of the most densely populated states in the US, but it still offers plenty of outdoor places to explore. In the northern part of the state you can visit the Appalachian and Kittatinny Mountains. In the central part of the state, Pinelands National Reserve features nearly a million acres of forests, wetlands, and farmlands. Most of New Jersey's urban centers are found to the north; with Newark and Jersey City. To the central and western part of the state, you'll find smaller cities. In the south, there is the premier vacation destination on Jersey Shore.

If you want to get away from the city, consider a trip to the Delaware Water Gap National Recreational Area along the western border with Pennsylvania. Another popular destination is the High Point State Park where you can enjoy views of a spring-fed lake. For fishing, you want to head to Hacklebarney State Park. For woodland hiking, stop by the Wharton State Forest.

SUGGESTED NEW JERSEY RV TRIP

The biggest draw in New Jersey is the Atlantic Coast. Take an RV trip through the three main cities along this route. The trip covers about 53 miles and takes about an hour. Start your trip in what is viewed as the Las Vegas of the East Coast, Atlantic City.

You can enjoy a number of casinos at a beachfront location. However, there is plenty of activities to enjoy both indoors and outdoors. Visit the Absecon Lighthouse, at 171 feet it is the tallest nautical beacon in the city. Or you can take in examples of marine life at the Atlantic City Aquarium.

The second stop is Ocean City, about 31 minutes and 20 miles south. Throughout the summer this is a popular beach destination for families with 8 miles of beaches and a famous boardwalk. The most popular is Gillian's Wonderland Park dating back to 1929.

The last stop is Cape May. It is a 42-minute trip to cover the 33 miles. This is a well-preserved historic town that offers winery tours and excellent restaurants. Don't miss a stop by the Cape May Bird Observatory to see migratory birds. Or enjoy the views from the Cape May Point State Park and its lighthouse.

Suggested RV Parks

In Cape May there are two excellent options for staying over for a few days. The first is Seashore Campsites and RV Resort. This large park features 675 spaces. It is open from April to October at the cost of $36 to $78. It is pet-friendly and features the following amenities:

- ★ Internet
- ★ Restrooms and Showers
- ★ Laundry
- ★ ATM
- ★ RV Supplies
- ★ Metered LP Gas
- ★ Firewood
- ★ Ice
- ★ Worship Services
- ★ Snack Bar
- ★ Groceries
- ★ Onsite RV Services
- ★ Cable
- ★ Fishing Supplies
- ★ Heated Pool
- ★ Wading Pool
- ★ Horseshoes

- ★ Game Room
- ★ Playground
- ★ Outdoor Games
- ★ Pavilion
- ★ Tennis
- ★ Exercise Room
- ★ Mini Golf

Another option is the 240 space Depot, Travel Park. Open from May to October, this pet-friendly park costs $41 to $58 and features the following amenities:

- ★ Internet
- ★ Restrooms and Showers
- ★ Laundry
- ★ Metered LP Gas
- ★ Firewood
- ★ Ice
- ★ Onsite RV Service
- ★ Cable
- ★ Horseshoes
- ★ Playground
- ★ Pavilion

RV CAMPING AT NEW JERSEY STATE PARKS

AMENITIES

- • Typical Cost: $22-$25

- Water: No
- Electric: No
- Sewer: No
- Laundry: Rarely
- In/Out Rules: 14 night maximum initially then 7 nights in and 7 nights out.

NEW JERSEY STATE PARKS

- ❑ Allaire State Park (45 sites)
- ❑ Bass River State Forest (176 sites)
- ❑ Belleplain State Forest (169 sites)
- ❑ Brendan T. Byrne State Forest (82 sites)
- ❑ Cheesequake State Park (53 sites)
- ❑ Jenny Jump State Forest (22 sites)
- ❑ Parvin State Park (56 sites)
- ❑ Spruce Run Recreation Area (67 sites)
- ❑ Stephens State Park (40 sites)
- ❑ Stokes State Forest (82 sites)
- ❑ Swartswood State Park (65 sites)
- ❑ Voorhees State Park (47 sites)
- ❑ Wharton State Forest (50 sites)
- ❑ Worthington State Forest (69 sites)

(Credit – WorldGuides.com)

New Mexico is known as the Land of Enchantment, and it is easy to see why when you discover its unique landscapes and vibrant city cultures. In the northern part of the state, you'll find the scenic backdrop of the Sangre de Cristo Mountains that give way to the Chihuahuan Desert in the south. The center of the state is a fertile valley thanks to the Rio Grande River.

Perhaps one of the best outdoor experiences is a trip to the Gila Cliff Dwellings National Monument, Aztec Ruins National Monument or the Chaco Culture National Historical Park. All of these parks offer a stunning trip back into time to see how past civilizations lived in the region.

New Mexico is also home to several iconic towns. Perhaps the most popular is Santa Fe, which is full of history and culture. From Sante Fe, you can take the Turquoise Trail Scenic Byway to New Mexico's largest city, Albuquerque.

SUGGESTED NEW MEXICO RV TRIP

New Mexico is an iconic state full of breathtaking views. Take a 304 mile trip with about five and half hours driving time to see all that this state has to offer while spending your days enjoying activities in five separate towns.

Your trip stars in Gallup along the historic Route 66 and the town celebrates this well. There are plenty of art galleries and shops along with a number of historic museums. A must see is the Navajo Code Talker Museum, which shows how the Native American language helped win World War II. You can also find a number of lovely murals while traveling through the historic Gallup Arts & Cultural District.

SUGGESTED RV PARK

In Gallup, you can choose to stay at the USA RV Park. This pet-friendly park features 126 spaces year round at the cost of $30 to $36 with the following amenities:

- ★ Internet
- ★ Restrooms and Showers
- ★ Laundry
- ★ RV Supplies
- ★ Metered LP Gas
- ★ Ice
- ★ Groceries
- ★ Restaurant
- ★ Onsite RV Service
- ★ Cable
- ★ Heated Pool
- ★ Horseshoes
- ★ Game Room
- ★ Playground
- ★ Outdoor Games
- ★ Putting Green

Your second stop is in Albuquerque. The trip is 146 miles down the road and takes about two hours along historic Route 66. Albuquerque is the largest city in New Mexico and features a number of attractions. The Old Town has been around since the Spanish founded the city in the early 1700s.

Be sure to take a ride on the Sandia Peak Tramway, with beautiful views of the city underneath you. You should also stop by the Petroglyph National Monument where you can hike through protected landscapes to see volcanoes, architectural sites and over 20,000 drawings that reflect native culture.

SUGGESTED RV PARKS IN ALBUQUERQUE

The surrounding area around the town is home to two wonderful RV parks where you can stay while you take a few days to explore all the area has to offer. The first is the Enchanted Trails RV Park and Trading Post. This park is open all year with 135 pet-friendly spaces at the cost of $34 to $37 with the following amenities:

★ Internet
★ Restrooms and Showers
★ Laundry
★ RV Supplies
★ Metered LP Gas
★ Ice
★ Onsite RV Service
★ Heated Pool
★ Hot Tub
★ Horseshoes
★ Recreation Hall
★ Game Room
★ Pavilion

Another option is the Route 66 RV Resort. This park features 100 spaces and is open all year. It costs $35 to $60 and is pet-friendly with an enclosed dog run and dog park along with the following amenities:

- ★ Internet
- ★ Restrooms and Showers
- ★ Laundry
- ★ ATM
- ★ RV Supplies
- ★ Ice
- ★ Restaurant
- ★ Cocktail Lounge
- ★ Guest Services
- ★ Heated Pool
- ★ Hot Tub
- ★ Water Slide
- ★ Horseshoes
- ★ Recreation Hall
- ★ Pavilion
- ★ Exercise Room
- ★ Pickle Ball

Santa Fe is the next stop about 64 miles down the road at a trip of about an hour. This is the state capital that dates back to 1607. Be sure to stop by the Museum of International Folk Art and the Palace of the Governors, one of the oldest continuously occupied structures in the United States.

While in Santa Fe you should take a free bird walk at the Randall Davey Audubon Center. This 135-acre sanctuary is an easy walk on rolling hills and forests. Another option for the outdoors is to visit the Santa Fe National Forest with over 1.6 million acres of trails. Lastly, stop by the Santa Fe Railyard; a 10-acre park with xeric gardens and a children's play area.

SUGGESTED RV PARK IN SANTA FE

With so much to see and do in this area, you should consider staying at the Santa Fe Skies RV Park. This smaller park has 98 spaces and is pet-friendly with a dog park. It is open all year at the cost of $37 to $46. It comes with the following amenities:

- ★ Internet
- ★ Restrooms and Showers
- ★ Laundry
- ★ RV Supplies
- ★ Metered LP Gas
- ★ Ice
- ★ Onsite RV Service
- ★ Recreation Hall
- ★ Game Room
- ★ Pavilion
- ★ Nature Trails

Your next stop is the town of Taos, about 70 miles down the road and takes about an hour and a half to get there. This town hosts a large art scene. There are also several historic sites to visit including the San

Francisco de Asis Mission Church as well as the Taos Pueblo, continuously inhabited for over a millennium.

Lastly, end your trip to the town of Angel Fire. This is a short 41-minute drive of about 24 miles down the road. This is a popular destination for the outdoor enthusiasts. It is known for mountain recreation as well as the towns Wild West history.

In the summer you can enjoy zip-lining, fly fishing, golfing, mountain biking and hiking; in the winter you can enjoy skiing and snowboarding. To enjoy the Wild West history be sure to use Roadrunner Tours for a horse-drawn wagon ride with a traditional dinner under the open sky.

SUGGESTED RV PARK IN ANGEL FIRE

At the end of your trip if you want to take a little break to enjoy the scenery for a few days, consider staying at the Angel Fire RV Resort. This park is open year-round with 102 spaces at the cost of $59 to $70. It is pet-friendly with a dog park and the following amenities:

★ Internet
★ Restrooms and Showers
★ Laundry
★ RV Supplies
★ Cable
★ Guest Services
★ Heated Pool
★ Hot Tub
★ Horseshoes

★ Recreation Hall

★ Pavilion

★ Nature Trails

★ Pickle Ball

★ Putting Green

RV CAMPING AT NEW MEXICO STATE PARKS

AMENITIES

- Typical Cost: $8-$18
- Water: Often (18 out of 30 parks)
- Electric: Usually (27 out of 30 parks)
- Sewer: Sometimes (9 out of 30 parks)
- In/Out Rules: 14 days maximum out of 20.

NEW MEXICO STATE PARKS

- ❏ Bluewater Lake (149 sites, 14 electric)
- ❏ Bottomless Lakes (37 sites, 32 electric)
- ❏ Brantley Lake (51 sites, 48 water & electric, 3 full hookups)
- ❏ Caballo Lake (170 sites, 108 water & electric, 7 full hookups)
- ❏ Cimarron Canyon (94 sites)
- ❏ City of Rocks (52 sites, 6 water & electric, 4 full hookups)
- ❏ Clayton Lake (26 sites, 7 water, 9 water & electric)
- ❏ Conchas Lake (105 site, 40 water & electric)
- ❏ Coyote Creek (47 sites, 19 electric, 15 water & electric)
- ❏ Eagle Nest Lake (19 sites)
- ❏ Elephant Butte Lake (173 sites, 144 water & electric, 8 full hookups)

- ❏ El Vado Lake (80 sites, 17 water & electric, 2 full hookups)
- ❏ Fenton Lake (5 water & electric)
- ❏ Heron Lake (250 sites, 54 electric)
- ❏ Hyde Park Memorial (50 sites, 7 electric)
- ❏ Leasburg Dam (31 sites, 16 water & electric)
- ❏ Manzano Mountains (23 sites, 9 electric)
- ❏ Morphy Lake (24 sites)
- ❏ Navajo Lake (244 sites, 41 electric, 56 water & electric, 8 full hookups)
- ❏ Oasis (29 sites, 10 water, 17 water & electric, 2 full hookups)
- ❏ Oliver Lee Memorial (44 sites, 16 water & electric)
- ❏ Pancho Villa (79 sites, 75 electric)
- ❏ Percha Dam (50 sites, 29 water & electric, 1 full hookup)
- ❏ Rockhound (29 sites, 23 electric)
- ❏ Santa Rosa Lake (75 sites, 25 electric)
- ❏ Storrie Lake (45 sites, 22 water & electric)
- ❏ Sugarite Canyon (40 sites, 8 water & electric, 2 full hookups)
- ❏ Sumner Lake (50 sites, 16 water & electric, 16 electric)
- ❏ Ute Lake (142 sites, 77 water & electric)
- ❏ Villanueva (33 sites, 12 electric)

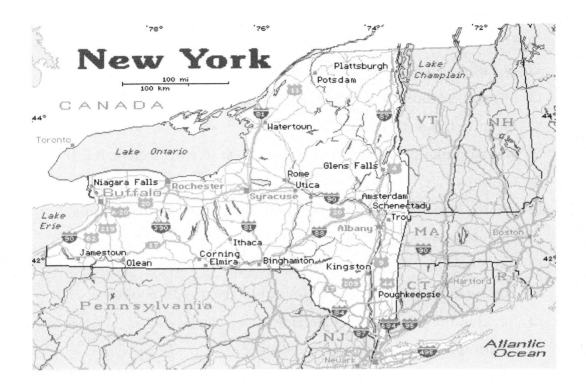

When most people think if New York they think of the city, but there is much more to see in the rest of the state. While there are plenty of things to see and do in the city, there are also plenty of enjoyable stops outside the city. Second to the city in tourist destinations is Niagara Falls.

New York is home to the largest preserved parcel of public land in the Adirondack Park in Upstate New York. This area is home to mountains, valleys, and lakes. To the north, you'll find Lake Placid where you can explore the history of the 1932 and 1980 Winter Olympics that were held here.

In the central part of the state, you'll find the Finger Lakes region. These rocky hillsides are filled with hidden waterfalls. There are several state parks in this area that offer a range of hiking, biking, and outdoor adventures. The best is Watkins Glen State Park with 19 waterfalls.

Of course, visiting New York City will give you so many iconic sights to see you're unlikely to see them all. There is the lush Central Park, skyscrapers with observation decks and the theaters of Broadway. Other iconic sites include the Statue of Liberty and the National 9/11 Memorial and Museum. There are plenty of museums and art galleries to explore for days.

SUGGESTED NEW YORK RV TRIP

Most people travel to New York to visit the big city and while there is plenty to see and do in the city; the true nature of New York comes out in a different road trip you can take in your RV. In less than 100 miles you can travel through Revolutionary history and spectacular scenes of nature in about an hour and a half drive.

Start your trip in the foothills of the Adirondacks at Saratoga Springs. This town is known as both a horse-racing venue and the healing thermal waters located here. Most people flock here in the summer during the Saratoga Race Course, but you can find plenty to do by coming here year round.

The second stop on your trip is at Lake George, about 31 minutes and 28 miles down the road. This town is a popular summer getaway for families, but it is also a great place to experience the great outdoors. Boating and swimming on the lake are popular activities, but you can also hike the 3.2-mile Prospect Mountain trail or take a hot-air balloon trip. Water Slide World is a great family destination with over 35 slides and other water activities.

While in the area there is plenty of free activities to enjoy. Stop by the Warren County Fish Hatchery to see a number of displays, plus enjoy an outdoor picnic area. You can also visit the Hyde Collection Art Museum that includes a historic house and art museum to teach about the heritage of the Adirondacks. Enjoy another piece of history by visiting Cooper's Cave Overlook to see how things looked with James Fennimore Cooper wrote Last of the Mohicans.

Take a visit to Valley Road Maple Farm to see a demonstration on how maple production happens while enjoying some free samples. Or you can visit Gore Mt. Farm to see how alpacas are raised and what products are made from their wool. Lastly be sure to check out Chapman Historical Museum to see what it was like to live in the area over 100 years ago.

SUGGESTED RV PARK

If you need more time to explore this area, then consider staying at Lake George RV Park. This large park has 368 pet-friendly spaces with a dog park, an enclosed dog run, and dog grooming. It is open May through October at the cost of $68 to $105 and features the following amenities:

- ★ Internet
- ★ Restrooms and Showers
- ★ Laundry
- ★ ATM
- ★ RV Supplies
- ★ Metered LP Gas

- ★ Firewood
- ★ Ice
- ★ Groceries
- ★ Restaurant
- ★ Onside RV Service
- ★ Cable
- ★ Guest Services
- ★ Self-Service RV Wash
- ★ Fishing Supplies
- ★ Golf Carts
- ★ Heated Pool
- ★ Wading Pool
- ★ Fishing Pond
- ★ Paddle Boats
- ★ Horseshoes
- ★ Recreation Hall
- ★ Game Room
- ★ Playground
- ★ Outdoor Games
- ★ Pavilion
- ★ Tennis
- ★ Shuffleboard
- ★ Exercise Room
- ★ Nature Trails
- ★ Bike Rentals
- ★ Lawn Bowling
- ★ Pickle Ball

The last stop in the trip is Fort Ticonderoga, about an hour down the road or about 56 miles. This town features a French-built fort along the banks of Lake Champlain that goes back to the Seven Years' War in the 18th century. For many years this fort was in ruins until 1908 when it was opened as a tourist attraction. Today you'll find a wide range of exhibits and the chance to see a historic reenactment.

RV CAMPING AT NEW YORK STATE PARKS

AMENITIES

- Typical Cost: $12-$51
- Water: Rarely (Only available at 4 parks)
- Electric: Rarely (Only available at 3 parks)
- Sewer: Rarely (Only available at 3 parks)
- In/Out Rules: From July 1st through Labor Day there is a 14-day maximum. Outside of this time, you may get extensions if availability allows.

NEW YORK STATE PARKS

The following parks have RV hookups:

- ❏ Cedar Point State Park (40 full hookup sites)
- ❏ Golden Hill State Park (52 water & electric sites)
- ❏ Taconic / Copake Falls (33 water only sites)
- ❏ Wellesley Island State Park (288 full hookup sites)
- ❏ Wildwood State Park (193 full hookup sites)
- ❏

PRIMITIVE FACILITY STATE PARKS

The following parks have primitive sites only:

- ❏ Allegany (245 sites)
- ❏ Ausable Point (141 sites)
- ❏ Bowman Lake (141 sites)
- ❏ Green Lakes (127 sites)
- ❏ Gilbert Lake (135 sites)
- ❏ Verona Beach (46 sites)
- ❏ Chenango Valley (178 sites)
- ❏ Fillmore Glen (60 sites)
- ❏ Oquaga Creek (90 sites)
- ❏ Delta Lake (101 sites)
- ❏ Glimmerglass (36 sites)
- ❏ Buttermilk Falls State Park (45 sites)
- ❏ Taughannock Falls State Park (34 sites)
- ❏ Robert H. Treman (64 sites)
- ❏ Bear Spring Mountain (25 sites)
- ❏ Cayuga Lake State Park (264 sites)
- ❏ Sampson (299 sites)
- ❏ Selkirk Shores State Park (143 sites)
- ❏ Watkins Glen (148 sites)
- ❏ Max V. Shaul (21 sites)
- ❏ Beaverkill (83 sites)
- ❏ Fair Haven Beach (173 sites)
- ❏ Little Pond Campground (68 sites)
- ❏ Caroga Lake Campground (156 sites)
- ❏ Newton Battlefield (12 sites)
- ❏ Whetstone Gulf State Park (57 sites)

- ❏ Mongaup Pond (154 sites)
- ❏ Keuka Lake (132 sites)
- ❏ Point Comfort Campground (63 sites)
- ❏ Little Sand Point Campground (58 sites)
- ❏ Nicks Lake Campground (101 sites)
- ❏ Poplar Point Campground (19 sites)
- ❏ Fish Creek Pond Campground (302 sites)
- ❏ Forked Lake Campground (5 sites)
- ❏ Four Mile Creek (258 sites)
- ❏ Gilbert Lake (135 sites)
- ❏ Golden Beach Campground (159 sites)
- ❏ Grass Point (70 sites)
- ❏ Green Lakes (126 sites)
- ❏ Hamlin Beach (251 sites)
- ❏ Hearthstone Point (174 sites)
- ❏ Higley Flow (128 sites)
- ❏ Hithers Hills (153 sites)
- ❏ Jacques Cartier (88 sites)
- ❏ Keewaydin (36 sites)
- ❏ Kenneth L. Wilson (66 sites)
- ❏ Keuka Lake (132 sites)
- ❏ Kring Point (73 sites)
- ❏ Lake Durant (52 sites)
- ❏ Lake Eaton (110 sites)
- ❏ Lake Erie (98 sites)
- ❏ Lake George Battleground Campground (57 sites)
- ❏ Lake Harris Campground (70 sites)
- ❏ Lake Taghkanic (8 sites)
- ❏ Lakeside (268 sites)

- ❑ Letchworth (258 sites)
- ❑ Lewey Lake Campground (177 sites)
- ❑ Limekiln Lake Campground (199 sites)
- ❑ Lincoln Pond Campground (18 sites)
- ❑ Little Pond Campground (61 sites)
- ❑ Little Sand Point Campground (56 sites)
- ❑ Long Point State Park (77 sites)
- ❑ Luzerne Campground (144 sites)
- ❑ Macomb Reservation State Park (95 sites)
- ❑ Max V. Shaul State Park (18 sites)
- ❑ Meacham Lake Campground (146 sites)
- ❑ Meadowbrook Public Campground (20 sites)
- ❑ Mills-Norrie State Park (42 sites)
- ❑ Moffitt Beach Campground (194 sites)
- ❑ Moreau Lake State Park (141 sites)
- ❑ Newton Battlefield State Park (12 sites)
- ❑ North-South Lake Campground (207 sites)
- ❑ Northampton Beach Campground (158 sites)
- ❑ Paradox Lake Campground (41 sites)
- ❑ Point Comfort Campground (43 sites)
- ❑ Poplar Point Campground (5 sites)
- ❑ Putnam Pond (44 sites)
- ❑ Robert Moses State Park (196 sites)
- ❑ Rogers Rock Campground (232 sites)
- ❑ Rollins Pond Campground (245 sites)
- ❑ Sacandaga Campground (125 sites)
- ❑ Sampson State Park (299 sites)
- ❑ Scaroon Manor Campground (55 sites)
- ❑ Sharp Bridge Campground (16 sites)

- ❏ Southwick Beach State Park (100 sites)
- ❏ Stony Brook State Park (80 sites)
- ❏ Taconic State Park (9 sites)
- ❏ Taylor Pond Campground (20 sites)
- ❏ Thacher State Park (131 sites)
- ❏ Westcott Beach State Park (154 sites)
- ❏ Wilmington Notch (41 sites)
- ❏ Woodland Valley (51 sites)

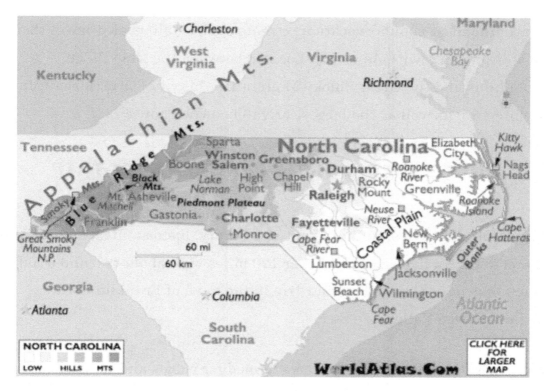

(Credit – www.worldAtlas.com)

The beauty that is North Carolina starts on the western border with the Appalachian Blue Ridge and the Great Smoky Mountains; which dominate the skyline. To the east, you'll find rolling hills and several cities within the Piedmont region. The cities of Raleigh, Durham and Chapel Hill form what is known as the Research Triangle. As you reach the shores of the Atlantic Ocean, you'll find several beautiful coastal towns of Wilmington, Beaufort, and New Bern.

One of the most popular scenic drives in America is the Blue Ridge Parkway. This drive runs parallel with the state's western border and covers some 500 miles. The state offers just as much coastline with nearly 300 miles of beaches.

One of the most popular vacation retreats in the state is also one of their most beautiful towns, Asheville. Located between the Blue Ridge Mountains and the Great Smoky Mountains, this city features beautiful architecture as well as the largest privately owned house.

SUGGESTED NORTH CAROLINA RV TRIP

North Carolina is a state full of natural beauty, historic sites, and urban centers. Take a five-city trip of over 120 miles with about two and a half hours of driving time. Start your trip in the town of Franklin in the historic Cowee Valley.

For generations this valley has been mined for rubies and sapphires, you can still mine for these gems in the many mines and mineral museums in the area. The outdoors also offer their own gems of beautiful waterfalls ranging from 60 to 250 feet along Route 64. The top three waterfalls you need to see are Bridal Veil, Dry and Cullasaja Falls.

SUGGESTED RV PARK

While in the area consider spending a night or two at The Great Outdoors RV Resort. This is a small and quaint RV park with 63 pet-friendly spaces that are open year-round at the cost of $49 to $55. While here you can enjoy the following amenities:

★ Internet

- ★ Restrooms and Showers
- ★ Laundry
- ★ RV Supplies
- ★ Metered LP Gas
- ★ Firewood
- ★ Ice
- ★ Groceries
- ★ Cable
- ★ Self-Service RV Wash
- ★ Swimming Pool
- ★ Recreation Hall
- ★ Exercise Room

Your second stop is the town of Cherokee about 41 minutes and 32 miles down the road. This town serves as the gateway to the Great Smoky Mountains National Park and a major part of American history.

Learn the story of the local Cherokee Indian tribe at the Museum of the Cherokee Indian. Just before entering the national park you'll find the hidden gem of Mingo Falls, a beautiful 200-foot cascading waterfall.

SUGGESTED RV PARK IN CHEROKEE

Spend a little extra time enjoying the nature in the area by staying a few nights at the RV Park Yogi in the Smokies. This rustic RV Park features 135 sites that are open all year at the cost of $39 to $76. The park is pet-friendly and features the following amenities:

- ★ Internet
- ★ Restrooms and Showers

- ★ Laundry
- ★ RV Supplies
- ★ Metered LP Gas
- ★ Firewood
- ★ Ice
- ★ Groceries
- ★ Fishing Supplies
- ★ Heated Pool
- ★ Horseshoes
- ★ Game Room
- ★ Playground
- ★ Outdoor Games
- ★ Pavilion
- ★ Nature Trails
- ★ Pedal Carts
- ★ Bike Rentals

The third stop in your trip is the mountain retreat of Lake Junaluska. It takes about 41 minutes to travel about 36 miles to this destination. The town was founded in the 1900s by the Methodist Church with the goal of relaxation. The lake features a 3.8-mile trail with a number of resting and viewing areas as well as several lavish gardens.

The fourth stop is the urban city of Asheville. It is a 27 mile trip of about 31 minutes. This city is home to one of the Southeast's best art scenes but has plenty of other things to see and do no matter what your interests. Nearby you can enjoy the great outdoors of Pisgah National Forest. This park is home to Looking Glass Falls, a waterfall of 60 feet that resembles a mirror in the winter.

Suggested RV Park in Ashville

While in the area there is another good RV park to stay at, the Asheville Bear Creek RV Park. This 114 site RV Park is open all year at the cost of $50 to $66. It is pet-friendly with a few amenities:

★ Internet
★ Restrooms and Showers
★ Laundry
★ RV Supplies
★ Metered LP Gas
★ Ice
★ Onsite RV Service
★ Cable
★ Heated Pool
★ Horseshoes
★ Recreation Hall
★ Playground
★ Outdoor Games

The last stop in the trip is the small town of Chimney Rock in the foothills of the Blue Ridge Mountains. This trip takes you about 45 minutes to travel 25 miles. Here you'll find one of the best examples of a human-made lake with Lake Lure. The park itself is known for the famed Chimney Rock featured in many films. Nearby, you'll find the famous Rainbow Falls; a 150-foot waterfall that is known for the rainbow that appears in the mist.

RV CAMPING AT NORTH CAROLINA STATE PARKS

AMENITIES

- Typical Cost: $17-$22
- Water: Not Usually
- Electric: Not Usually
- Sewer: No
- In/Out Rules: 14 nights out of 30.

NORTH CAROLINA STATE PARKS

- ❏ Falls Lake State Recreation Area (176 water & electric sites, 99 primitive sites)
- ❏ Jordan Lake State Recreation Area (690 water & electric sites, 1000 total sites)
- ❏ Kerr Lake State Recreation Area (342 water & electric sites, 700 total sites)
- ❏ Carolina Beach State Park (80 sites)
- ❏ Cliffs of the Neuse State Park (30 sites)
- ❏ Jones Lake State Park (20 sites)
- ❏ Merchants Millpond State Park (20 sites)
- ❏ Medoc Mountain State Park (34 sites, 12 water & electric)
- ❏ Pettigrew State Park (13 sites)
- ❏ Hanging Rock State Park (70 sites)
- ❏ Lake Norman State Park (30 sites)
- ❏ Morrow Mountain State Park (100 sites)
- ❏ Pilot Mountain State Park (50 sites)
- ❏ Stone Mountain State Park (40 sites)

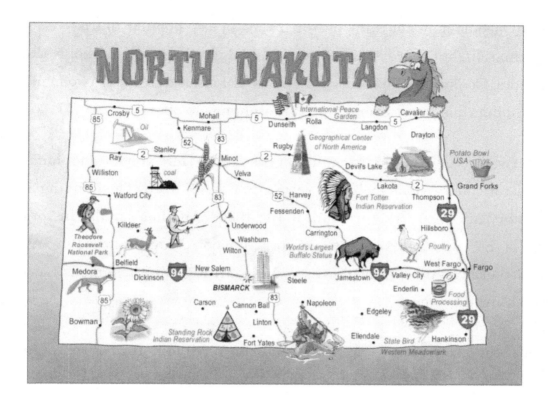

(Credit – Western Meadowlark)

North Dakota offers a diverse landscape with plenty of outdoor activities. This state allows you to travel the same path as Lewis and Clark. Two wonderful stops include the Theodore Roosevelt National Park and the Peace Garden which offers you a number of historic sites and museums.

Despite the desolate landscape, there are still several cities to explore. Fargo is located on the Red River in the eastern portion of the state and offers a rich cultural and historical experience. Or you can visit the state capital of Bismarck located in the central part of the state.

SUGGESTED NORTH DAKOTA RV TRIP

Many people may not think of North Dakota as a popular tourist destination, but there is plenty to see and do in the great state of North Dakota. Consider a three-city RV trip of 119 miles and about two hours of driving time to see everything this state has to offer.

Start your trip in the state capital of Bismarck. Here you'll find a number of historic attractions including the State Capitol itself. The building is a 19-story Art Deco structure built in the 1930s. Another popular historic site is the Victorian Former Governors Mansion State Historic Site. Also, make sure you take a ride down the Missouri River in the famous Lewis and Clark Riverboat.

The second stop on the trip is the Audubon Wildlife Refuge about an hour down the road or about 65 miles. This area is a wonderful expanse of prairie and wetlands that is home to a number of migratory birds along with a range of mammals and reptiles. The refuge is also home to a visitor center and a mile long nature trail or the eight-mile South Shore Auto Tour Route.

The last stop in the trip is the town of Minot about another hour down the road or about 54 miles. The must-see destination here is the Scandinavian Heritage Park. This is an open-air museum with full-scale replicas of Nordic buildings from all five Scandinavian countries. The most popular building is the Norwegian Gol Stave Church, a copy of a medieval pinewood house dating back to the 13th century. Take the time to enjoy an authentic Finnish sauna or enjoy north European foods.

RV CAMPING AT NORTH DAKOTA STATE PARKS

AMENITIES

- Typical Cost: $20
- Water: Sometimes
- Electric: Sometimes
- Sewer: Rarely
- In/Out Rules: 14 out of 30 nights

NORTH DAKOTA STATE PARKS

- ❏ Beaver Lake (31 sites)
- ❏ Cross Ranch (65 sites)
- ❏ Lewis and Clark (87 water & electric)
- ❏ Fort Ransom (25 electric)
- ❏ Turtle River (125 water & electric)
- ❏ Shelvers Grove State Recreation Area (26 full hookups)
- ❏ Grahams Island (144 full hookups)
- ❏ Lake Metigoshe State Park (125 water & electric)
- ❏ Fort Abraham Lincoln State Park (95 water & electric)
- ❏ Little Missouri State Park (25 electric)
- ❏ Sully Creek State Recreation Area (37 sites)
- ❏ Doyle Memorial State Park (varied sites)
- ❏ Indian Hills State Recreation Area and Resort (water & electric)
- ❏ Lake Sakakawea State Park (192 water & electric)
- ❏ Fort Stevenson State Park (145 full hookups)

Ohio is at the crossroads between the northeast region and the Midwest, making Ohio known for its nickname the Heart of It All. It features three big cities: Cincinnati, Cleveland, and Columbus. It also features a number of outdoor adventures at popular destinations such as Lake Erie and the Appalachian Mountains.

Southeastern Ohio is home to the Appalachian Mountains, and the best destination is Wayne National Forest. Another option is the Hocking Hills, State Park. At the Cuyahoga Valley National Park, you will find natural areas mixed with urban environments.

The capital and largest city in Ohio is Columbus. Then along the shores of Lake Erie, you'll find Cleveland, the second-largest city of Ohio. This city is known for its distinctive public parks and nature preserves. Here you'll also find the top attraction in the state, the Rock and Roll Hall of Fame.

Along the southern shore of Lake Erie, you'll find Cedar Point, which is considered one of the best theme parks in the United States. It was started in 1870 and is now a huge amusement park featuring a number of attractions.

SUGGESTED OHIO RV TRIP

Ohio is the perfect place for an RV trip since it offers a combination of family-friendly activities, outdoor adventures, and excellent museums. Get the full experience by traveling along the shores of Lake Erie in a 124 mile trip of about two hours.

Your trip starts out in Sandusky, known for Cedar Point; one of the most famous amusement parks in the United States. This park features roller-coasters, five of which are over 200 meters in height. Other attractions in the area include a speedway, a deer park and a number of water parks. If you want to head outdoors, you can take advantage of a number of fishing opportunities.

SUGGESTED RV PARKS

While in the area there are two excellent RV parks to choose from. The first is Milan Travel Park. This small park of 85 sites is open from May to November at the cost of $42. It is pet-friendly with the following amenities:

- ★ Internet
- ★ Restrooms and Showers
- ★ Laundry
- ★ RV Supplies
- ★ Metered LP Gas
- ★ Firewood
- ★ Ice
- ★ Onsite RV Service
- ★ Swimming Pool
- ★ Game Room
- ★ Playground
- ★ Pavilion
- ★ Shuffleboard
- ★ Nature Trails

The other option is Camp Sandusky. This park is open from May to October with 115 sites that cost between $30 to $69. It is a pet-friendly park with the following amenities:

- ★ Internet
- ★ Restrooms and Showers
- ★ Laundry
- ★ Firewood
- ★ Ice
- ★ Groceries
- ★ Onsite RV Service

- ★ Heated Pool
- ★ Playground
- ★ Outdoor Games
- ★ Pavilion
- ★ Pedal Carts

Your second stop is the urban city of Cleveland. It is about an hour drive to cover the 66 miles. Cleveland is located on the banks of Lake Erie and is the second-largest city in Ohio. The biggest attraction here is the Rock and Roll Hall of Fame. Other must-see attractions in the area include the Cleveland Botanical Garden, the Cleveland Museum of Art and the Cleveland Aquarium.

The third and final stop is the small town of Ashtabula, located 58 miles and about an hour down the road. This town is known for its scenic terrain and world-class wineries. You'll also be able to walk across a number of historic covered bridges, some over centuries old. Two ideal options are the Middle Road Covered Bridge in Conneaut dating back to 1868 and the Olin Covered Bridge dating back to 1873.

RV CAMPING AT OHIO STATE PARKS

AMENITIES

- Typical Cost: $18-$38
- Water: Sometimes (13 out of 54 parks)
- Electric: Often (36 out of 54 parks)
- Sewer: Sometimes (13 out of 54 parks)
- In/Out Rules: 14 out of 30.

- ❏ Mt. Gilead (54 electric sites)
- ❏ Delaware (176 electric sites)
- ❏ Alum Creek (252 full hookups)
- ❏ Malabar Farm (15 primitive sites)
- ❏ Mohican (156 full hookups)
- ❏ Indian Lake (444 full hookups)
- ❏ Van Buren (61 electric sites)
- ❏ Findley (254 electric sites)
- ❏ Kiser Lake (65 electric sites)
- ❏ Buck Creek (95 electric sites)
- ❏ Dillon (169 electric sites)
- ❏ Muskingum River (19 primitive sites)
- ❏ East Harbor (485 full hookups)
- ❏ A.W. Marion (48 electric sites)
- ❏ Deer Creek (20 electric sites)
- ❏ Kelley's Island (93 electric sites)
- ❏ Mary Jane Thurston (35 electric sites)
- ❏ John Bryan (53 electric sites)
- ❏ South Bass Island (62 full hookups)
- ❏ Lake Loramie (124 electric sites)
- ❏ Grand Lake St. Mary's (194 full hookups)
- ❏ Maumee Bay (224 electric sites)
- ❏ Portage Lakes (69 electric sites)
- ❏ Blue Rock (97 sites)
- ❏ Great Seal (25 sites)
- ❏ Hocking Hills (169 electric sites)

- ❏ Tar Hollow (83 electric sites)
- ❏ Salt Fork (252 full hookups)
- ❏ Sycamore (15 primitive sites)
- ❏ Caesar Creek (245 electric sites)
- ❏ Burr Oak (93 electric sites)
- ❏ Lake Hope (190 electric sites)
- ❏ Paint Creek (156 electric sites)
- ❏ Scioto Trail (47 electric sites)
- ❏ Cowan Lake (220 electric sites)
- ❏ Wolf Run (128 electric sites)
- ❏ Pike Lake (79 electric sites)
- ❏ Harrison Lake (177 electric sites)
- ❏ Rocky Fork (124 full hookups)
- ❏ Lake Alma (70 electric sites)
- ❏ West Branch (184 full hookups)
- ❏ Barkcamp (138 electric sites)
- ❏ Stonelick (95 electric sites)
- ❏ Punderson (111 full hookups)
- ❏ Guilford Lake (36 electric sites)
- ❏ Jefferson Lake (45 primitive sites)
- ❏ Hueston Woods (345 electric sites)
- ❏ East Fork (341 full hookups)
- ❏ Forked Run (145 electric sites)
- ❏ Beaver Creek (56 electric sites)
- ❏ Mosquito Lake (177 electric sites)
- ❏ Shawnee (88 electric sites)
- ❏ Geneva (79 full hookups)
- ❏ Pymatuning (279 full hookups)

Presenting...

OKLAHOMA

Within the state of Oklahoma, you'll find a dozen different ecosystems with a wide variety of terrain. Lakes and rivers have expanses of shoreline while other parts of the state are home to cypress swamps and thick forests. You'll also notice a rich history of Wild West culture in this state at their heritage centers, museums, and outfitters. You'll also find 39 Native American tribe headquarters in this state.

Oklahoma features 33 state parks to keep you busy outdoors. The best place to start is at the Red Rock Canyon State Park, the ideal place to go hiking. Another option is the Robbers Cave State Park, located in the Sans Bois Mountains to the east. Head to the northeast for your water sports at the Grand Lake O' the Cherokees. This reservoir covers 46,500 acres and nearly 1,300 miles of shoreline.

For an urban experience unlike any other, Oklahoma City offers you a big city experience with old-fashioned Western charm. Here you will find the National Cowboy and Western Heritage Museum with its impressive collection of Western art and artifacts. For more modern art and culture head to Tulsa, the second largest city in the state.

SUGGESTED OKLAHOMA RV TRIP

When it comes to an RV road trip, the first thing that comes to mind is the historic Route 66. Oklahoma features the longest drivable portion of Route 66 over any other state. Take in all that Oklahoma has to offer with a three-city stop of 191 miles that takes you about three hours to drive with plenty of roadside attractions.

Start your trip out in Tulsa, with some interesting attractions. Tulsa is the second-largest city in Oklahoma. Here you'll find unique roadside attractions such as the 75-foot high Golden Driller; a statue of an oil worker that dates back to the 1950s. Other must-sees include the Route 66 Village, an open-air museum full of restored train cars and a 194-foot high oil derrick.

After you've finished Tulsa, head about an hour and a half down the road the 106 miles to get to the urban center of Oklahoma City. In this capital city, you'll find a number of attractions that include the National Cowboy and Western Heritage Museum and the Oklahoma History Center. You should also stop by the free Route 66 Park that features a watchtower, an amphitheater, and wetlands.

SUGGESTED RV PARK

If you need a little extra time exploring all there is to see along this three-city route, consider staging in the middle at the Roadrunner RV Park. This 132 space park is open all year at the cost of $36 to $38. It is pet-friendly with the essential amenities including:

★ Internet
★ Restrooms and Showers
★ Laundry
★ Ice
★ Cable
★ Recreation Hall
★ Playground

The last stop on the trip is the town of Clinton. It is 85 miles down the road and takes about an hour to get there. This small little town is full of attractions to see. Consider the Mohawk Lodge Indian Store, a small museum that features Native American craft items. The main attraction is the Oklahoma Route 66 Museum that traces the history of this famous roadway.

RV CAMPING AT OKLAHOMA STATE PARKS

AMENITIES

• Typical Cost: $12-$30

- Water: Yes
- Electric: Yes
- Sewer: Often (20 out of 37 parks)
- Laundry: Sometimes
- In/Out Rules: 14 nights with extensions available on request.

OKLAHOMA STATE PARKS

- ❏ Little Sahara (86 water & electric)
- ❏ Alabaster Caverns (22 water & electric)
- ❏ Grand Lake (215 water & electric)
- ❏ Beavers Bend & Hochatown (87 water & electric)
- ❏ Roman Nose (12 full hookups, 35 water & electric)
- ❏ Robbers Cave (22 full hookups, 67 water & electric)
- ❏ Sequoyah Bay (71 water & electric)
- ❏ Lake Texoma (88 full hookups, 41 water & electric)
- ❏ Osage Hills (20 water & electric)
- ❏ Raymond Gary (100 full hookups, 9 water & electric)
- ❏ Lake Thunderbird (30 full hookups, 170 water & electric)
- ❏ Great Plains (14 full hookups, 38 water & electric)
- ❏ Tenkiller (85 water & electric, some with full hookups)
- ❏ Great Salt Plains (1 full hookup, 63 water & electric)
- ❏ Keystone (72 full hookups)
- ❏ Foss (10 full hookups, 100 water & electric)
- ❏ Greenleaf (100 water & electric, some with full hookups)
- ❏ Cherokee Landing (93 water & electric)
- ❏ Talimena (10 water & electric)
- ❏ Red Rock Canyon (44 full hookups, 44 water & electric, 26 primitive)

- ❏ Lake Murray (329 full hookups)
- ❏ Okmulgee (47 water & electric, 1 full hookup)
- ❏ Natural Falls (17 full hookups, 27 water & electric)
- ❏ Clayton Lake (30 water & electric)
- ❏ Lake Wister (118 water & electric)
- ❏ Fort Cobb (7 full hookups, 284 water & electric)
- ❏ Dripping Springs (76 water & electric)
- ❏ Black Mesa (36 water & electric)
- ❏ Boiling Springs (40 water & electric)
- ❏ McGee Creek (100 water & electric)
- ❏ Sequoyah (48 full hookups, 80 water & electric)
- ❏ Arrowhead (20 full hookups, 71 water & electric)
- ❏ Lake Eufaula (34 full hookups, 65 water & electric)

Oregon is a state surrounded by water with the Pacific Ocean on one side and the Columbia River to the north. This state has no shortage of natural beauty and wonderful outdoor experiences.

If you visit during low tide, head to Haystack Rock. This beach in the central coast area features an iconic monolith that stands 235 feet while at its base you will see tide pools with an abundance of local flora and fauna.

To the north is the Columbia River and the Cascade Range. Here you'll find the 600-foot waterfall at Multnomah Falls. A historic bridge allows you to hike in front of the falls. To the southeast is the stunning Crater

Lake National Park with a caldera formed by a volcanic mountain collapse some 7,700 years ago. It now forms the deepest lake in the United States at 1,943 feet. You can take the 33 mile Rim Drive to see the scenic points and geological features, or you can take a ranger-led boat tour.

Among the natural beauty, you'll find the beautiful town of Portland. This hip town offers plenty of things to do and taste.

To truly experience all that Oregon has to offer, consider a drive along the Pacific Coast Scenic Byway. Here you can enjoy sweeping ocean views while passing through several small seaside towns from Astoria to Coos Bay. You'll also be able to explore a number of lighthouses along this route.

SUGGESTED OREGON RV TRIP

The Columbia River is Oregon is rich in beauty and history. Take a long 312 mile trip to four cities along this ideal RV trip to see all that Oregon has to offer. It will take you about five and a half hours to drive with a few recommended stops along the way so you can enjoy all the area has to offer.

Start your trip out in the town of Pendleton. This is a town that is focused on Wild West heritage. If you are there in early September, you'll want to stay for the Pendleton Round-Up, a highlight of the rodeo circuit.

SUGGESTED RV PARK IN PENDLETON

While in the area, especially if you are going to stay for the Round-Up, you'll want to stay at the Wildhorse Resort & Casino RV Park. This 100 space park is open year-round at the cost of $30 to $45. It is pet-friendly with the following amenities:

★ Internet
★ Restrooms and Showers
★ Laundry
★ Metered LP Gas
★ Ice
★ Snack Bar
★ Groceries
★ Restaurant
★ Self-Service RV Wash
★ Heated Pool
★ Hot Tub
★ Horseshoes
★ Golf
★ Driving Range
★ Exercise Room
★ Putting Green

The second stop takes you about two hours to drive 131 miles down the road to The Dalles. This destination is on the banks of the Columbia River with plenty of outdoor adventure opportunities. Be sure to visit the Columbia Gorge Discovery Center where you can really study the history of Lewis and Clark. You will also find a number of exhibits focused on the local Native American culture and basketry.

Your third stop is the town of Portland. It will take you about an hour and a half to travel the 80 miles to this town. The town itself is known for dining spots, coffee shops, and boutiques. However, there is still plenty to enjoy outdoors. Be sure to visit Forest Park located on the Willamette River; you'll find over 80 miles of manicured trails at this largest urban park in the United States.

SUGGESTED RV PARK IN PORTLAND

Spend a little time at this midpoint of your trip at the Jantzen Beach RV Park. This 169 space RV Park is open all year at the cost of $35. It is pet-friendly with the following amenities:

★ Internet
★ Restrooms and Showers
★ Laundry
★ Cable
★ Self-Service RV Wash
★ Heated Pool
★ Wading Pool
★ Horseshoes
★ Recreation Hall
★ Game Room
★ Playground
★ Exercise Room

Your trip ends in the small town of Astoria. It is 101 miles down the road and takes you about two hours to get there. Astoria is an authentic fishing village located on the rugged coastline. A must see is Fort Clatsop, the outpost of Lewis and Clark when they reached the Pacific Ocean. This area is also popular with Hollywood films, and you'll notice a lot of distinctive scenery.

RV CAMPING AT OREGON STATE PARKS

AMENITIES

- Typical Cost: $10-$32
- Water: Usually (43 out of 46 parks)
- Electric: Often (32 out of 46 parks)
- Sewer: Often (22 out of 46 parks)
- In/Out Rules: 14 nights in, 3 nights out.

OREGON STATE PARKS

- ❑ Ainsworth (40 full hookups)
- ❑ Alfred A. Loeb (45 water & electric)
- ❑ Beachside State Recreation Site (30 water & electric)
- ❑ Beverly Beach (53 full hookups)
- ❑ Bullards Beach (100 full hookups, 82 water & electric)
- ❑ Cape Blanco (50 water & electric)
- ❑ Cape Lookout (35 full hookups)
- ❑ Carl G. Washburne (500 full hookups, 5 water & electric)
- ❑ Catherine Creek (20 primitive sites)
- ❑ Champoeg (8 full hookups, 67 water & electric)

- ❏ Clyde Holliday State Recreation Site (30 water & electric)
- ❏ Collier Memorial (10 full hookups)
- ❏ Deschutes River State Recreation Area (34 water & electric)
- ❏ Detroit Lake (105 full hookups, 98 water & electric)
- ❏ Devil's Lake State Recreation Area (25 full hookups)
- ❏ Emigrant Springs State Heritage Area (18 full hookups, 1 water & electric)
- ❏ Fall Creek State Recreation Area (39 primitive sites)
- ❏ Farewell Bend State Recreation Area (90 water & electric)
- ❏ Fort Stevens (170 full hookups, 300 water & electric)
- ❏ Goose Lake State Recreation Area (45 water & electric)
- ❏ Harris Beach (35 full hookups, 50 water & electric)
- ❏ Hilgard Junction (18 primitive sites)
- ❏ Humbug Mountain (40 water & electric)
- ❏ Jasper Point (30 water & electric)
- ❏ Jessie M. Honeyman Memorial (45 full hookups, 120 water & electric)
- ❏ Joseph H. Stewart State Recreation Area (150 water & electric)
- ❏ L.L. Stub Stewart (88 full hookups)
- ❏ LaPine (80 full hookups, 45 water & electric)
- ❏ Lake Owyhee (29 water & electric)
- ❏ Memaloose (40 full hookups)
- ❏ Milo McIver (44 water & electric)
- ❏ Minam State Recreation Area (40 water only)
- ❏ Nehalem Bay (265 water & electric)
- ❏ Prineville Reservoir (22 full hookups, 20 water & electric)
- ❏ Red Bridge State Wayside (10 primitive sites)
- ❏ Silver Falls (116 water & electric)
- ❏ South Beach (225 water & electric)

- ❏ Sunset Bay (30 full hookups, 35 water & electric)
- ❏ Cove Palisades (85 water & electric)
- ❏ Tumalo (23 full hookups)
- ❏ Umpqua Lighthouse (10 full hookups, 9 water & electric)
- ❏ Unity Lake (35 water & electric)
- ❏ Valley of the Rogue (85 full hookups, 59 water & electric)
- ❏ Viento (55 water & electric)
- ❏ Wallowa Lake (121 full hookups)
- ❏ William M. Tugman (94 water & electric)

PENNSYLVANIA

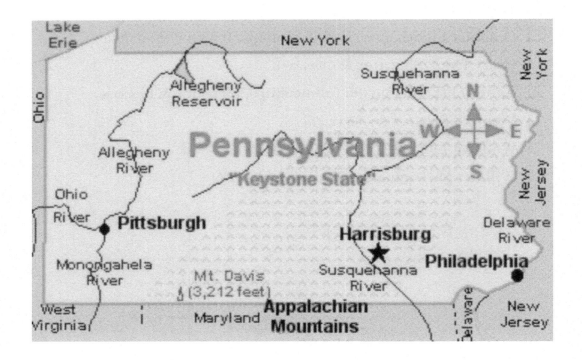

Pennsylvania has played a major role in US history, more than any other state. Philadelphia's Independence Hall is where the Declaration of Independence was signed in 1776. For a short-term, the city served as the capital and home to the first president, George Washington. Pennsylvania later served as the turning point of the Civil War and still later as the major steel producer during the industrialization of the United States.

When you visit the largest city in Pennsylvania, Philadelphia, you are stepping back in time. However, you can also experience a good deal of history in the city of Erie, located along the southern shore of Lake Erie. For beautiful views of the waters be sure to head out to Presque Isle State Park.

SUGGESTED PENNSYLVANIA RV TRIP

Take a three-city trip through Pennsylvania to explore some of the most historic places in the United States. It is a short trip of about 55 miles and only takes about an hour and a half to drive, but there is plenty to see and do to keep you busy.

Start your trip in the historic Gettysburg. The Gettysburg National Military Park is where the pivotal Battle of Gettysburg happened during the Civil War. This part is commemorated with a number of monuments. Take the time to visit the Gettysburg Museum of the Civil War to see relics and interactive exhibits. For the shopper, you can stop by at Artifact at 777 to purchase relics and artwork from the 1800s and earlier.

SUGGESTED RV PARK

If you want to take more time and stay in the area consider stopping by Gettysburg Campground. This 240 site park is open from March to November at the cost of $43 to $72. This pet-friendly RV Park features the following amenities:

- ★ Internet
- ★ Restrooms and Showers
- ★ Laundry
- ★ ATM
- ★ RV Supplies
- ★ Metered LP Gas
- ★ Firewood
- ★ Ice
- ★ Snack Bar

- ★ Groceries
- ★ Onsite RV Service
- ★ Cable
- ★ Guest Services
- ★ Fishing Supplies
- ★ Swimming Pool
- ★ Horseshoes
- ★ Recreation Hall
- ★ Game Room
- ★ Playground
- ★ Outdoor Games
- ★ Pavilion
- ★ Shuffleboard
- ★ Pedal Carts
- ★ Mini Golf

The second stop in this historic trip is the town of York. It is a drive of about 29 miles and takes about 59 minutes. This is the place to go if you want to see how things get built. York is a small town featuring a number of manufacturing plants that offer public tours. Some worthwhile stops include the Harley-Davidson Vehicle Operations Factory, Martin's Potato Chips, and Wolfgang Candy Company.

SUGGESTED RV PARK

Need a place to stay over in the middle of this trip? Consider Tucquan Park Family Campground. This park has 155 spaces open all year at the cost of $43 to $47. It is pet-friendly with the following amenities:

- ★ Internet
- ★ Restrooms and Showers
- ★ Laundry
- ★ ATM
- ★ RV Supplies
- ★ Metered LP Gas
- ★ Firewood
- ★ Ice
- ★ Snack Bar
- ★ Groceries
- ★ Onsite RV Service
- ★ Self-Service RV Wash
- ★ Fishing Supplies
- ★ Swimming Pool
- ★ Fishing Pond
- ★ Paddle Boats
- ★ Horseshoes
- ★ Recreation Hall
- ★ Game Room
- ★ Playground
- ★ Outdoor Games
- ★ Pavilion
- ★ Nature Trails

The final stop in the trip is the town of Lancaster. It is a short 26 miles and about 38-minute drive down the road. This town is the center of Pennsylvania Dutch Country and gives you a glimpse at the Amish way of life. Be sure to visit the Amish Village where you can see a 12-acre

Amish cultural attraction complete with a one-room schoolhouse, an 1840 farmhouse, and a local market.

You can also visit the Cherry Crest Adventure Farm with 50 family-friendly activities that include things like pedal carts, wagon tours, and a petting zoo.

RV CAMPING AT PENNSYLVANIA STATE PARKS

AMENITIES

- Typical Cost: $17-$39
- Water: Often (44 out of 53 parks)
- Electric: Usually (only 7 parks are primitive)
- Sewer: Usually (10 out of 53 parks)
- In/Out Rules: From Memorial to Labor day 14 days, 21 days otherwise.

PENNSYLVANIA STATE PARKS

The following state parks offer full hookups:

- ❏ Black Moshannon (74 sites)
- ❏ Hills Creek (87 sites)
- ❏ Gifford Pinchot (289 sites)
- ❏ French Creek (200 sites)
- ❏ Hickory Run (380 sites)
- ❏ Promised Land (256 sites)
- ❏ Cook Forest (215 sites)
- ❏ Kooser (35 sites)

- ❏ Laurel Hill (260 sites)
- ❏ Pymatuning (400 sites)

The following state parks have electric hookups only:

- ❏ Bald Eagle (167 sites)
- ❏ Chapman (80 sites)
- ❏ Hyner Run (30 sites)
- ❏ Kettle Creek (71 sites)
- ❏ Leonard Harrison (25 sites)
- ❏ Little Pine (99 sites)
- ❏ Lyman Run (36 sites)
- ❏ Ole Bull (79 sites)
- ❏ Parker Dam (109 sites)
- ❏ Poe Valley (50 sites)
- ❏ Raymond B. Winter (58 sites)
- ❏ Sinnemahoning (35 sites)
- ❏ Sizerville (23 sites)
- ❏ Blue Knob (50 sites)
- ❏ Caledonia (178 sites)
- ❏ Codorus (193 sites)
- ❏ Colonel Denning (52 sites)
- ❏ Cowans Gap A (204 sites)
- ❏ Fowlers Hollow (18 sites)
- ❏ Greenwood Furnace (51 sites)
- ❏ Little Buffalo (40 sites)
- ❏ Pine Grove Furnace (70 sites)
- ❏ Prince Gallitzin (400 sites)
- ❏ Shawnee (260 sites)

- ❏ Trough Creek (29 sites)
- ❏ Frances Slocum (100 sites)
- ❏ Lackawanna (90 sites)
- ❏ Locust Lake (280 sites)
- ❏ Worlds End (70 sites)
- ❏ Clear Creek (53 sites)
- ❏ Keystone (90 sites)
- ❏ Ohiopyle (200 sites)
- ❏ Raccoon Creek (184 sites)
- ❏ Ryerson Station (45 sites)

PRIMITIVE CAMPING SITES AT STATE PARKS

The following state parks offer primitive camping only:

- ❏ Cherry Springs (30 sites)
- ❏ Colton Point (25 sites)
- ❏ Patterson (10 sites)
- ❏ Poe Paddy (34 sites)
- ❏ Simon B. Elliott (25 sites)
- ❏ Ricketts Glen (120 sites)
- ❏ Tobyhanna (140 sites)

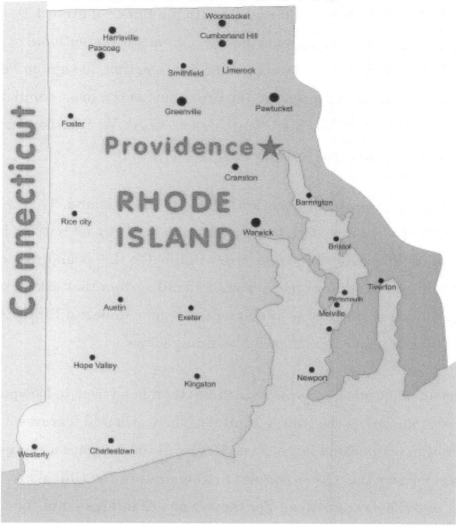

Rhode Island is a quick RV trip since it only takes you 45 minutes to drive through the state. However, don't rush; rather take your time to settle down and look at all the things the state has to offer you. Rhode Island offers you over 400 miles of coastline with beaches, jagged cliffs, and lighthouses. However, beyond this beautiful waterfront, you will also find a number of quaint villages, vineyards and bustling cities.

If it is beach time, you want then head to Narragansett Bay. This is a beautiful area comprised of 30 islands with a number of protected harbors and inlets to provide you plenty of areas for recreational activities. Enjoy the area on your own or take the time to sign up for seal-watching tours or boat cruises. In the area some of the most popular beaches include East Matunuck State Beach, Roger W. Wheeler State Beach and Narragansett Town Beach.

For a truly unique outdoor experience head to Block Island. This is located 12 miles off the south coast and is accessible by ferry. This island is home to rolling hills, cliffs, and rare wildlife. On this island, you can visit the Block Island Conservancy with a trail system that takes you through a diverse range of wildlife and the scenic Mohegan Bluffs that towers 200 feet above the ocean for stunning views.

If an urban experience is more your thing, then head over to Newport. This city is known as the sailing capital of the world and features a number of mansions and large estates. A lot of these homes are museums and open for viewing. Other popular attractions are the Cliff Walk, Ford Adams, and the Jazz Festival. For those who are interested in the creative arts, you want to visit Providence. This city is home to a number of art, music and culinary options.

SUGGESTED RHODE ISLAND RV TRIP

Rhode Island is a small state, but still well worth an RV trip. Take a three-city trip of about 63 miles in a little over an hour of driving time to witness the history, heritage, and beauty of the state of Rhode Island.

Start your trip out in Providence, home of Brown University and capital of the state of Rhode Island. The city places a big emphasis on water, and while there you should experience Water Fire, an award-winning incendiary sculpture that is located on the city's downtown river.

The second stop is the town of Narragansett, about a 45 minute or 29 mile trip down the road. This town features some of the best beaches in New England. Be sure to stop by Point Judith Lighthouse that has been standing for over 100 years. Also be sure to check out Fishermen's Memorial State Park, a 91-acre preserve and campground.

The last stop in the trip is the town of Westerly. It is again about a 35-minute trip to travel the 35 miles. This is a popular family destination. A must see is the Flying Horse Carousel, a historic ride dating back to the 1800s. Also be sure to stop by the Atlantic Beach Park where you can take in a variety of oceanfront fun.

RV CAMPING AT RHODE ISLAND STATE PARKS

AMENITIES

- Typical Cost: $20-$35
- Water: Rarely (1 out of 4 parks)

- Electric: Rarely (1 out of 4 parks)
- Sewer: Rarely (1 out of 4 parks)
- In/Out Rules: In the summer the max is 14 days. The rest of the year is extended to 21 days. In both situations, you have to be out 7 days before returning.

RHODE ISLAND STATE PARKS

- ❏ Burlingame State Park (900 primitive sites)
- ❏ Charlestown Breachway (75 primitive sites)
- ❏ Fishermen's State Park and Campground (182 sites, 40 full hookups)
- ❏ George Washington Memorial Camping Area (45 primitive sites)

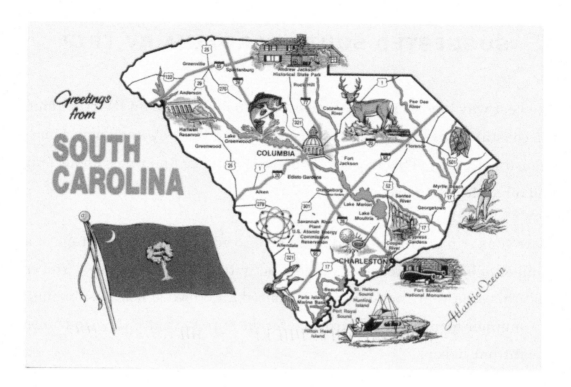

No trip to South Carolina is complete without taking a drive into the high peaks of the Blue Ridge Mountains and the low hills of the Piedmont region. This state also has a strong Old South heritage that rings out in plenty of historic sites as well as modern urban centers.

In the heart of South Carolina, you'll find the town of Charleston. Here you'll be able to walk cobblestone streets that are still towered over by church steeples. Take the time to join a walking tour that teaches you about the colonial past and beautiful architecture of the city.

If you visit the coast be sure to stop by Myrtle Beach, which offers some of the most beautiful beaches along the Atlantic coast. Here you will find family attractions, shopping destinations, amusement parks, music shows and any number of outdoor recreational options.

SUGGESTED SOUTH CAROLINA RV TRIP

The best way to visit and see South Carolina is to take an RV trip along the coastal areas. Visit three main cities along the way and enjoy some beautiful scenery. This trip covers about 208 miles and takes about four and a half hours to drive.

Start your trip at Hilton Head Island. Here you can take advantage of a number of beautiful beaches, outdoor activities, and golf courses. You can visit this area year round, but be prepared for crowded beaches during the summer months. If you are a golfer, be sure to visit Palmetto Dunes Oceanfront Resort.

The second stop on the trip is the urban center of Charleston. It is about a two-hour drive to get the 113 miles down the road. Charleston is one of the oldest cities in the United States, dating back to 1670. The town is known for its variety of architecture including Georgian, Antebellum and Victorian. Be sure to visit the 17th century Old Exchange and Provost Dungeon building as well as the historic seawall promenade of the Battery. Another must-see is the 1676 Magnolia Plantation and Gardens.

SUGGESTED RV PARKS

While at this midpoint of your trip there are two excellent RV parks you can choose to stay at. The first is Oak Plantation Campground. It is a large 220 site park that is open all year at the cost of $45 to $53. It is pet-friendly with an enclosed dog run as well as the following amenities:

★ Internet
★ Restrooms and Showers
★ Laundry
★ RV Supplies
★ Metered LP Gas
★ Firewood
★ Ice
★ Worship Services
★ Cable
★ Self-Service RV Wash
★ Swimming Pool
★ Fishing Pond
★ Horseshoes
★ Playground
★ Outdoor Games
★ Pavilion
★ Frisbee Golf

Another option is to stay at The Campground at James Island County Park. This is a smaller park with 124 sites. It is open all year at the cost of $44 to $55. Pets are welcome at this park that features the following amenities:

★ Internet
★ Restrooms and Showers
★ Laundry

- ★ RV Supplies
- ★ Metered LP Gas
- ★ Firewood
- ★ Ice
- ★ Snack Bar
- ★ Groceries
- ★ Fishing Supplies
- ★ Fishing Pond
- ★ Boat Rentals
- ★ Paddle Boats
- ★ Horseshoes
- ★ Recreation Hall
- ★ Playground
- ★ Outdoor Games
- ★ Pavilion
- ★ Nature Trails
- ★ Bike Rentals
- ★ Frisbee Golf

Your trip ends in the town of Myrtle Beach. It is about a two-hour drive to cover the 96 miles to the town. This is one of the most popular beach destinations on the East Coast of the United States. Be sure to stop by Ripley's Aquarium and WonderWorks, an adventure park for the whole family with rope courses, laser tag, and sea life exhibits. For a more adult experience, visit the Art Museum of Myrtle Beach or the Burning Ridge Golf Club.

RV CAMPING AT SOUTH CAROLINA STATE PARKS

AMENITIES

- Typical Cost: $15-$19
- Water: Usually
- Electric: Usually
- Sewer: Sometimes
- In/Out Rules: Maximum of 14 days.

SOUTH CAROLINA STATE PARKS

- ❏ Andrew Jackson (25 water & electric)
- ❏ Baker Creek (100 water & electric)
- ❏ Barnwell (25 full hookups)
- ❏ Calhoun Falls State Recreation Area (86 water & electric)
- ❏ Cheraw (18 water & electric)
- ❏ Chester (27 water & electric)
- ❏ Colleton (25 water & electric)
- ❏ Croft State Natural Area (50 water & electric)
- ❏ Devil's Fork (82 water & electric)
- ❏ Dreher Island State Recreation Area (112 water & electric)
- ❏ Edisto Beach (125 water & electric)
- ❏ Givhans Ferry (25 water & electric)
- ❏ H. Cooper Black (27 water & electric)
- ❏ Hamilton Branch (200 water & electric)
- ❏ Hickory Knob State Resort Park (44 water & electric)
- ❏ Hunting Island (200 water & electric)
- ❏ Huntington Beach (133 full hookups)

- ❏ Keowee-Toxaway State Natural Area (24 water & electric)
- ❏ Kings Mountain (125 water & electric)
- ❏ Lake Greenwood (125 water & electric)
- ❏ Lake Hartwell (117 water & electric)
- ❏ Lake Wateree State Recreation Area (72 water & electric)
- ❏ Lee (48 water & electric)
- ❏ Little Pee Dee (50 water & electric)
- ❏ Myrtle Beach (300 full hookups)
- ❏ Oconee (155 water & electric)
- ❏ Paris Mountain (39 water & electric)
- ❏ Poinsett (50 water & electric)
- ❏ Sadlers Creek (66 water & electric)
- ❏ Santee (188 water & electric)
- ❏ Sesquicentennial (87 water & electric)
- ❏ Table Rock (110 water & electric)

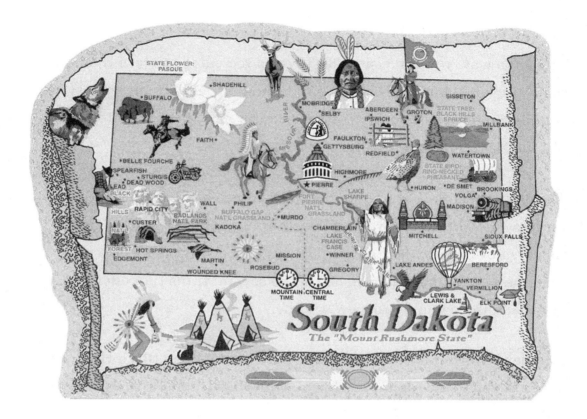

Along the western edge of the Great Plains, you'll come across the state of South Dakota which is home to several large monuments such as Mount Rushmore National Memorial and huge buffalo herds at Custer State Park. However, there is just as much to see in small towns such as Custer and Deadwood or urban centers such as Sioux Falls and Rapid City.

visit from Brandon

Perhaps the most iconic trip in South Dakota is a trip along I-90. Along this trip you'll see a number of beautiful landscapes ranging from open prairies to the towering peaks of the Black Hills. Plus you can view a number of iconic stops along the way. Your trip starts out in Sioux Falls, the largest city in South Dakota. Here you'll find a number of walking and hiking trails throughout the city. Two great stops are the Great Plains Zoo and the Butterfly House and Aquarium.

Along the way, you can visit 1880 Town, a recreated western community consisting of 30 buildings housing thousands of relics from the past. As you continue, you'll come to another historic spot at the Minuteman Missile National Historic Site.

The best outdoor experience in South Dakota is at Badlands National Park in the southwest corner of the state. You can take a brief tour of this area by driving the Badlands Loop Road. Or you can spend more time there and take a hike on one of the several trails that offer different views and the potential to view wildlife.

Another beautiful natural area in South Dakota is the Black Hills. This is where you'll find Mount Rushmore which is visited by over three million people a year. The Black Hills is also home to Custer State Park at over 70,000 acres. In this park, you'll see a variety of wildlife including bison, prairie dogs, pronghorn and feral burros.

SUGGESTED SOUTH DAKOTA RV TRIP

South Dakota is a state that packs a lot to see on a short road trip. Visit five historic cities along a 91 miles stretch of road that takes about two hours to drive. Along the way, you'll have plenty to keep you busy for days.

Start your trip in the small town of Custer at the center of South Dakota's Black Hills National Forest. At this park, you must see a number of important destinations including Mount Rushmore, Crazy Horse Memorial, Devils Tower, Black Hills, and Badlands. Also be sure to stop by Custer State Park where you can see majestic bison and burros.

The second stop on your trip is Hill City. It is a short 19-minute drive to cover the 14 miles to this destination. This little town is at the geographic center of the Black Hills and provides you with plenty to do. At one time it was a mining center and today is a main staging area for visiting Mount Rushmore. Be sure to ride the restored 1880 train and take a spelunking tour of Wind Cave.

SUGGESTED RV PARK

Consider spending a few days to enjoy the area at Rafter J Bar Ranch Camping Resort. This 180 site park is open from May to October at the cost of $46 to $68. It is pet-friendly with the following amenities:

★ Internet
★ Restrooms and Showers
★ Laundry
★ ATM
★ RV Supplies
★ Metered LP Gas
★ Firewood
★ Ice
★ Snack Bar
★ Groceries

- ★ Onsite RV Service
- ★ Guest Services
- ★ Fishing Supplies
- ★ Heated Pool
- ★ Hot Tub
- ★ Playground
- ★ Outdoor Games
- ★ Pavilion
- ★ Nature Trails

Your third stop is the city of Rapid City. It is a short 35-minute drive to cover the 27 miles. This town puts you between the Black Hills and the Badlands. It offers you small town charm with big city adventures. Be sure to visit Dinosaur Park to see life-size dinosaur replicas.

SUGGESTED RV PARK

If you need to spend more time in the area, then be sure to check out Rushmore Shadows Resort. This 198 space park is open from May to October at the cost of $44 to $64. It is pet-friendly with the following amenities:

- ★ Internet
- ★ Restrooms and Showers
- ★ Laundry
- ★ RV Supplies
- ★ Firewood
- ★ Ice
- ★ Groceries
- ★ Guest Services

- ★ Heated Pool
- ★ Hot Tub
- ★ Horseshoes
- ★ Game Room
- ★ Playground
- ★ Outdoor Games
- ★ Pavilion
- ★ Tennis
- ★ Nature Trails
- ★ Bike Rentals
- ★ Mini Golf
- ★ Pickle Ball

The second to the last stop is the town of Sturgis. It takes about 30 minutes to drive the 28 miles. Since 1938 this city has been home to the annual Sturgis Motorcycle Rally in August. There is still plenty to see and do in this area throughout the year.

End your trip in the small town of Spearfish. It is a drive of about 22 miles and takes about 23 minutes. The best activity here is sightseeing. There is plenty of water activities such as tubing and fly fishing. Plus there is plenty of activities in town to keep you busy as well.

RV CAMPING AT SOUTH DAKOTA STATE PARKS

AMENITIES

- Typical Cost: $11-$21
- Water: No
- Electric: Often

- Sewer: No
- In/Out Rules: 14 night maximum.

SOUTH DAKOTA STATE PARKS

The following state parks are prime camping with restrooms, showers, electric hookups, and waterfront sites:

❏ Chief White Crane Recreation Area (37 sites)
❏ Lewis & Clark Recreation Area (101 sites)

The following state parks have restrooms and showers, with most having electric hookups:

❏ Angostura Recreation Area (169 sites)
❏ Big Sioux Recreation Area (49 sites)
❏ Farm Island Recreation Area (90 sites)
❏ Hartford Beach (87 sites)
❏ Lake Cochrane Recreation Area (30 sites)
❏ Lake Herman (72 sites)
❏ Lake Louise (39 sites)
❏ Lake Poinsett (114 sites)
❏ Lake Thompson (103 sites)
❏ Lake Vermillion Recreation Area (94 sites)
❏ Mina Lake Recreation Area (36 sites)
❏ Newton Hills (128 sites)
❏ North Point Recreation Area (111 sites)
❏ Oahe Downstream Recreation Area (204 sites)
❏ Oakwood Lakes (136 sites)
❏ Palisades (34 sites)

- ❏ Pelican Lake Recreation Area (76 sites)
- ❏ Pickerel Lake Recreation Area (77 sites)
- ❏ Pierson Ranch Recreation Area (67 sites)
- ❏ Randall Creek Recreation Area (132 sites)
- ❏ Richmond Lake Recreation Area (24 sites)
- ❏ Rocky Point Recreation Area (66 sites)
- ❏ Roy Lake (100 sites)
- ❏ Sandy Shore Recreation Area (23 sites)
- ❏ Shadehill Recreation Area (56 sites)
- ❏ Snake Creek Recreation Area (115 sites)
- ❏ Springfield Recreation Area (20 sites)
- ❏ Walker's Point Recreation Area (43 sites)
- ❏ West Bend Recreation Area (127 sites)

STATE PARKS WITH LIMITED FACILITIES

The following state parks offer electric hookups, some with restrooms and showers:

- ❏ Buryanek Recreation Area (44 sites)
- ❏ Cow Creek Recreation Area (39 sites)
- ❏ Fisher Grove (22 sites)
- ❏ Fort Sisseton Historic State Park (14 sites)
- ❏ Indian Creek Recreation Area (124 sites)
- ❏ Okobojo Point Recreation Area (17 sites)
- ❏ Pease Creek Recreation Area (23 sites, 5 primitive sites)
- ❏ Platte Creek Recreation Area (36 sites)
- ❏ Swan Creek Recreation Area (26 sites)
- ❏ Union Creek (25 sites, 4 primitive sites)

❏ West Pollock Recreation Area (29 sites)

❏ West Whitlock Recreation Area (105 sites)

PRIMITIVE CAMPING SITES AT STATE PARKS

The following state parks are primitive only:

❏ Bear Butte State Park (23 sites)

❏ Burke Lake Recreation Area (15 sites)

❏ Lake Hiddenwood Recreation Area (13 sites)

❏ Llewellyn Johns Recreation Area (10 sites)

❏ North Wheeler Recreation Area (25 sites)

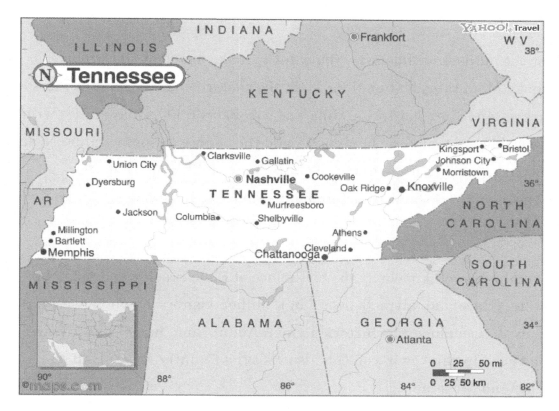

(Credit – www.maps.com)

Tennessee offers a range of stunning landscapes from the Mississippi Delta lowlands up to the towering peaks of the Great Smoky Mountains. Across these landscapes you'll find over 300 waterfalls that feed crystal-clear creeks and rivers; offering some excellent options for fishing, swimming, and other water activities.

Perhaps one of the most known parts of Tennessee is the music culture in Memphis and Nashville. Even the Appalachian region has its own music culture. Many music icons have their homes and studios open for tours such as Elvis Presley, Johnny Cash, and Dolly Parton. Other urban centers such as Chattanooga and Knoxville offers tourist options such as zoos, museums, entertainment scenes and plenty of cultural and historic sites.

For the outdoor enthusiasts, you want to make a stop at the Great Smoky Mountains National Park. At the eastern edge of the state, this park extends into North Carolina and covers over 800 square miles with natural beauty, historic landmarks and the chance to spot wildlife. Near the park, you'll find the towns of Gatlinburg and Pigeon that offer amusement parks and entertainment venues, so everyone is sure to find something.

Memphis is well known as the birthplace of Elvis Presley and today his estate, Graceland, attracts over a half million visitors a year. Then in Nashville, you have the historic Ryman Auditorium, home to the Grand Ole Opry. In this town, you can also visit the Country Music Hall of Fame and Museum.

SUGGESTED TENNESSEE RV TRIP

Tennessee not only features a number of fun urban centers, but it also has a fantastic natural skyline with the Great Smoky Mountains National Park. Take a trip to three beautiful cities to see all that Tennessee has to offer. It is a short trip of just about 14 miles that can be done in as little as 30 minutes but gives you plenty to see and do in the great outdoors.

Start your trip in the town of Sevierville, a popular family destination. Be sure to stop by the Smoky Mountain Deer Farm, the subterranean

Forbidden Caverns, and the NASCAR Speedpark. For adults, you can visit Eagle Springs Winery or tour the Tennessee Legend Distillery.

SUGGESTED RV PARKS IN SEVIERVILLE

If you need more time in the area, there are two excellent RV parks to choose from. The first is Ripplin' Waters Campground & Cabin Resort. This 156 site RV Park is open all year at the cost of $36 to $41. It is pet-friendly and comes with the following amenities:

- ★ Internet
- ★ Restrooms and Showers
- ★ Laundry
- ★ RV Supplies
- ★ Metered LP Gas
- ★ Firewood
- ★ Ice
- ★ Worship Services
- ★ Groceries
- ★ Self-Service RV Wash
- ★ Swimming Pool
- ★ Playground
- ★ Pavilion

Your other option is RV Plantation RV Resort. This is a larger park with 299 spaces open year round at the cost of $29 to $65. It is pet-friendly with a dog park and the following amenities:

- ★ Internet

- ★ Restrooms and Showers
- ★ Laundry
- ★ RV Supplies
- ★ Metered LP Gas
- ★ Firewood
- ★ Ice
- ★ Worship Services
- ★ Cable
- ★ Staffed RV Wash
- ★ Golf Carts
- ★ Swimming Pool
- ★ Hot Tub
- ★ Wading Pool
- ★ Recreation Hall
- ★ Game Room
- ★ Playground
- ★ Pavilion
- ★ Exercise Room
- ★ Frisbee Golf
- ★ Pickle Ball

The second stop in your trip is the town of Pigeon Forge. It is a short 7 mile trip of about 20 minutes down the road. This small town is an entertainment mecca with beautiful views of the Great Smoky Mountains.

Two of the most famous entertainment themed attractions here is the Elvis Presley Museum and Dollywood. Plus a must see is a replica of the Titanic ocean liner.

SUGGESTED RV PARKS PIGEON FORGE

With so much to see and do in the area, you can consider this as a staging area and stay at one of two excellent RV parks in the area. The first is King's Holly Haven RV Park. This 162 site RV Park is open all year at a rate of $27 to $39. It is pet-friendly and offers you the following amenities:

★ Internet
★ Restrooms and Showers
★ Laundry
★ RV Supplies
★ Firewood
★ Ice
★ Onsite RV Service
★ Cable
★ Self-Service RV Wash
★ Swimming Pool
★ Playground
★ Pavilion

Another option is the Riveredge RV Park and Log Cabin Rentals. This 175 site RV park is pet-friendly and open all year at the cost of $39 to $55. It offers you the following amenities:

★ Internet
★ Restrooms and Showers
★ Laundry
★ RV Supplies

* ★ Firewood
* ★ Ice
* ★ Onsite RV Service
* ★ Cable
* ★ Heated Pool
* ★ Hot Tub
* ★ Wading Pool
* ★ Game Room
* ★ Playground

The third and final stop on the trip is Gatlinburg. It is another short drive of 17 minutes to get about 7 miles to your destination. This town is your main gateway to the Great Smoky Mountains and is popular with outdoor enthusiasts.

The city is home to Ober Gatlinburg, the only ski resort in the state, and features its own aerial tramway with beautiful scenery in both the winter and summer. A must see is the Ripley Aquarium, home to a number of exotic sea life.

RV CAMPING AT TENNESSEE STATE PARKS

AMENITIES

* Typical Cost: $8-$28
* Water: Yes
* Electric: Yes
* Sewer: Rarely (4 out of 31 parks)
* Laundry: Sometimes
* In/Out Rules: 14 days maximum.

TENNESSEE STATE PARKS

- ❑ Big Ridge (50 water & electric)
- ❑ Bledsoe Creek (57 water & electric)
- ❑ Cedars of Lebanon (87 water & electric)
- ❑ Chickasaw (52 water & electric, 32 primitive sites)
- ❑ Cove Lake (106 water & electric)
- ❑ Cumberland Mountain (145 water & electric)
- ❑ David Crockett (115 water & electric)
- ❑ Davey Crockett Birthplace (88 water & electric, 54 full hookups)
- ❑ Edgar Evins (60 water & electric)
- ❑ Fall Creek Falls (222 water & electric, 92 full hookups)
- ❑ Harrison Bay (128 water & electric)
- ❑ Henry Horton (56 water & electric)
- ❑ Indian Mountain (47 water & electric)
- ❑ Meeman-Shelby Forest (49 water & electric)
- ❑ Montgomery Bell (40 water & electric, some full hookups)
- ❑ Mousetail Landing (25 water & electric)
- ❑ Natchez Trace (200 water & electric, 100 full hookups)
- ❑ Nathan Bedford Forrest (37 water & electric)
- ❑ Norris Dam (75 water & electric)
- ❑ Old Stone Fort (51 water & electric)
- ❑ Panther Creek (50 water & electric)
- ❑ Paris Landing (45 water & electric)
- ❑ Pickett (32 water & electric)
- ❑ Pickwick Landing (86 water & electric)
- ❑ Reelfoot Lake (86 water & electric)

- ❑ Roan Mountain (87 water & electric)
- ❑ Rock Island (60 water & electric)
- ❑ Standing Stone (36 water & electric)
- ❑ T.O. Fuller (45 water & electric)
- ❑ Tims Ford (52 water & electric)
- ❑ Warriors' Path (174 water & electric)

TEXAS

Texas is a state with so much to see and do that you likely won't get to do it in one trip. Rather take the time to do multiple RV trips through the state to see everything it has to offer. From a historic and cultural standpoint, Texas has belonged to six nations over the centuries. Texas is a state filled with natural beauty as well as fun urban areas.

For a truly rustic and natural experience you want to head to the border with Mexico. Here you can visit Big Bend National Park with a vast wilderness that spans a desert and a mountain range. This means you have a diverse range of plant and wildlife species to enjoy. At night the park offers some of the best stargazing anywhere.

Two wonderful Texas towns to visit include San Antonio and Austin. San Antonio is the second largest city in Texas and offers plenty of historic Spanish missions to tour as well as the famous River Walk entertainment district. Then there is the Alamo, which played an important part in Texas independence. In the town of Austin, there is a thriving art, music, and food culture.

SUGGESTED TEXAS RV TRIP

Texas is a vast and open state. In order to get a feel for all this state has to offer you should take a five-city circuit through Hill Country. It is about a 250-mile loop that takes you about five and a half hours to drive with lots to see and do along the way.

Start your trip in the third largest city in Texas, San Antonio. Perhaps best known as the 1836 sites of the Battle of Alamo, this city features a number of the excellent museum in Mission-style architecture. Be sure to take a gondola ride down the San Antonio River or take a walk down the River Walk.

The second stop on the loop is the town of Kerrville. It is about 66 miles away and takes you about an hour drive. This town is located on the Guadalupe River and is known for its beautiful parks and endless fields of bluebonnet flowers. Be sure to stop by the historic Captain Charles Schreiner Mansion; a 19th century old stone estate that houses the Hill

Country Museum. Another must see if you want to experience true Texan is the Kerrville Museum of Western Art.

The third stop is a short 31-minute drive down the road of about 24 miles to the town of Fredericksburg. This town is best known for German food, culture, and architecture. Be sure to visit the Pioneer Museum Complex, a living history museum with log cabins, a one-room schoolhouse, and a historic firehouse. While here you can also stop by the largest wildflower seed farm in the United States.

Your second to the last stop is the urban center of Austin. It takes about an hour and a half to drive the 78 miles to this capital city. It is known for its music scene, but there are plenty other things to do as well. Be sure to stop by the Congress Bridge, home to the biggest urban bat colony in North America. Also, stop by the Bullock Texas State History Museum to learn about the state's history.

SUGGESTED RV PARKS

While in the area, if you need more time consider two excellent RV parks to stay at. The first is Austin Lone Star RV Resort. This pet-friendly RV Park has 156 spaces and is open all year at the cost of $47 to $60. It offers you the following amenities:

- ★ Internet
- ★ Restrooms and Showers
- ★ Laundry
- ★ RV Supplies
- ★ Metered LP Gas
- ★ Ice

- ★ Groceries
- ★ Cable
- ★ Self-Service RV Wash
- ★ Heated Pool
- ★ Wading Pool
- ★ Horseshoes
- ★ Recreation Hall
- ★ Playground
- ★ Outdoor Games
- ★ Pavilion
- ★ Exercise Room

Another option is the La Hacienda Sun RV Resort. This large park features 346 spaces at a pet-friendly park open all year at a cost of $50 to $65 with the following amenities:

- ★ Internet
- ★ Restrooms and Showers
- ★ Laundry
- ★ RV Supplies
- ★ Metered LP Gas
- ★ Ice
- ★ Cable
- ★ Self-Service RV Wash
- ★ Heated Pool
- ★ Hot Tub
- ★ Horseshoes
- ★ Recreation Hall
- ★ Exercise Room

- ★ Nature Trails
- ★ Putting Green

The last stop in the loop is New Braunfels. It takes you about 50 minutes to drive the almost 48 miles. This town was founded in 1845 by German immigrants. Be sure to walk the Gruene Historic District, a preserved neighborhood with an original Texas dance hall. There is plenty of water activities along the Comal and Guadalupe Rivers. You can also spend time at the seasonal Schlitterbahn outdoor waterpark. Complete the loop by traveling 39 minutes or about 32 miles back to San Antonio.

RV CAMPING AT TEXAS STATE PARKS

AMENITIES

- Typical Cost: $8-$24
- Water: Usually (Only 5 out of 73 parks don't have water)
- Electric: Usually (Only 5 out of 73 parks don't have water)
- Sewer: Often (22 out of 73 parks have full hookups)
- In/Out Rules: Most parks are 14 in, 14 out. In the winter months, some parks allow for monthly stays.

TEXAS STATE PARKS

The following state parks have full hookups:

- ❑ Abilene
- ❑ Atlanta
- ❑ Bastrop
- ❑ Blanco

- ❏ Caddo Lake
- ❏ Cleburne
- ❏ Daingerfield
- ❏ Davis Mountains
- ❏ Eisenhower
- ❏ Falcon
- ❏ Fort Richardson, Lost Creek Reservoir State Trailway
- ❏ Goliad
- ❏ Lake Brownwood
- ❏ Lake Corpus Christi
- ❏ Lake Livingston
- ❏ Lake Whitney
- ❏ Lockhart
- ❏ McKinney Falls
- ❏ Meridian
- ❏ Mission Tejas
- ❏ Stephen F. Austin State Park
- ❏ Tyler

RV PARKS WITH LIMITED FACILITIES

The following state parks feature water and electric hookups:

- ❏ Balmorhea (has cable hookups)
- ❏ Bonham
- ❏ Brazos Bend
- ❏ Buescher
- ❏ Caprock Canyons Trailway
- ❏ Cedar Hill

- ❑ Choke Canyon
- ❑ Cooper Lake
- ❑ Copper Breaks
- ❑ Dinosaur Valley
- ❑ Fairfield Lake
- ❑ Fort Parker
- ❑ Galveston Island
- ❑ Garner
- ❑ Goose Island
- ❑ Guadalupe River
- ❑ Hueco Tanks SHS
- ❑ Huntsville
- ❑ Inks Lake
- ❑ Lake Arrowhead
- ❑ Lake Bob Sandlin
- ❑ Lake Casa Blanca
- ❑ Lake Colorado City
- ❑ Lake Mineral Wells Trailway
- ❑ Lake Somerville Trailway
- ❑ Lake Tawakoni
- ❑ Lake Texana
- ❑ Lost Maples SNA
- ❑ Martin Creek Lake
- ❑ Martin Dies, Jr.
- ❑ Monahans Sandhills
- ❑ Mother Neff
- ❑ Mustang Island
- ❑ Palmetto
- ❑ Palo Duro Canyon

- ❏ Pedernales Falls
- ❏ Possum Kingdom
- ❏ Purtis Creek
- ❏ Ray Roberts Lake
- ❏ San Angelo
- ❏ Sea Rim
- ❏ Seminole Canyon
- ❏ South Llano River
- ❏ Village Creek

PRIMITIVE CAMPING SITES AT STATE PARKS

The following state parks have primitive sites only:

- ❏ Big Bend Ranch
- ❏ Colorado Bend
- ❏ Devils River State Natural Area
- ❏ Franklin Mountains
- ❏ Hill Country State Natural Area

(Credit – www.facts.co)

Utah is well known for the red rock arches, and massive rock formations found in the desert terrain. This is why Utah is home to five national parks and eight national monuments. Much of the state is sparse, but the

Salt Lake metropolitan area is densely populated with nearly one million residents.

Most of Utah's national parks are connected by scenic byways that make for a beautiful RV trip. One of the top must-see destinations is Zion National Park in the southwest corner of the state. Here you can hike through slot canyons with red walls that tower thousands of feet above you. Just as beautiful is Arches National Park with the iconic red rock arch image that comes from the 65 foot tall Delicate Arch.

Salt Lake City is a popular destination for those wanting to experience the outdoors while also being close to historical and cultural offerings within the city. While here you can visit the Family History Library for genealogy research to find your family history.

SUGGESTED UTAH RV TRIP

Utah features a number of stunning natural landscapes. Consider a four-city RV trip that allows you to experience the best the state has to offer. It is a 252-mile trip that takes about four and a half hours to drive.

Start your trip in the town of St. George. This town places you within an hour's drive of Zion National Park. Within the city itself, there is a performing arts scene, an art museum, a children's museum and plenty of outdoor adventure opportunities. A must see family-friendly attraction is the Dinosaur Discovery Site at Johnson Farm with huge dinosaur tracks.

The second stop is about 140 miles down the road to Bryce and takes about two hours to get there. Once you're done visiting Zion National Park, the next stop is Bryce Canyon National Park with a number of unique geological structures. You'll find a number of hiking trails ranging from one to eleven miles.

About 76 miles down the road you come to the city of Boulder in about an hour and a half. Most choose to skip the town itself and go straight to Capitol Reef National Park. However, within the town itself, there are a number of other beautiful sites as well such as Calf Creek Falls, Anasazi State Park, and the Grand Staircase-Escalante National Monument.

The last stop in the trip is the town of Torrey. It is a short 51-minute drive to cover the 36 miles. This town is the perfect staging ground to visit the Capitol Reef National Park. At this park, you want to visit the Capitol Reef's Grand Wash and Capitol Gorge for a number of wonderful outdoor adventures.

RV CAMPING AT UTAH STATE PARKS

AMENITIES

- Typical Cost: $12-$35
- Water: Often (20 out of 33 parks)
- Electric: Often (23 out of 33 parks)
- Sewer: Sometimes (10 out of 33 parks)
- In/Out Rules: 14 days out of a 30 day period.

Utah State Parks

- ❑ Antelope Island (26 primitive sites)
- ❑ Bear Lake (143 sites, full hookups available)
- ❑ Coral Pink Sand Dunes (22 primitive sites)
- ❑ Dead Horse Point (21 electric sites)
- ❑ Deer Creek (53 sites, full hookups available)
- ❑ East Canyon (76 sites, full hookups available)
- ❑ Escalante Petrified Forest (22 water & electric sites)
- ❑ Fremont Indian (30 primitive sites)
- ❑ Goblin Valley (23 primitive sites)
- ❑ Goosenecks (primitive camping)
- ❑ Great Salt Lake (water & electric sites)
- ❑ Green River (36 electric sites)
- ❑ Gunlock (primitive sites)
- ❑ Huntington (22 primitive sites)
- ❑ Hyrum (32 water & electric sites)
- ❑ Jordanelle (144 water & electric sites)
- ❑ Kodachrome Basin (31 sites, full hookups available)
- ❑ Millsite (20 primitive sites)
- ❑ Otter Creek (53 electric sites)
- ❑ Palisades (76 sites, full hookups available)
- ❑ Piute (primitive sites)
- ❑ Quail Creek (23 primitive sites)
- ❑ Red Fleet (38 sites, full hookups available)
- ❑ Rockport (86 water & electric sites)
- ❑ Sand Hollow (67 sites, full hookups available)
- ❑ Scofield (water & electric sites)
- ❑ Snow Canyon (31 water & electric sites)

- ❏ Starvation (33 water & electric sites)
- ❏ Steinaker (31 sites, full hookups available)
- ❏ Utah Lake (71 water & electric sites)
- ❏ Wasatch Mountain (139 sites, full hookups available)
- ❏ Willard Bay (78 sites, full hookups available)
- ❏ Yuba (107 water & electric sites)

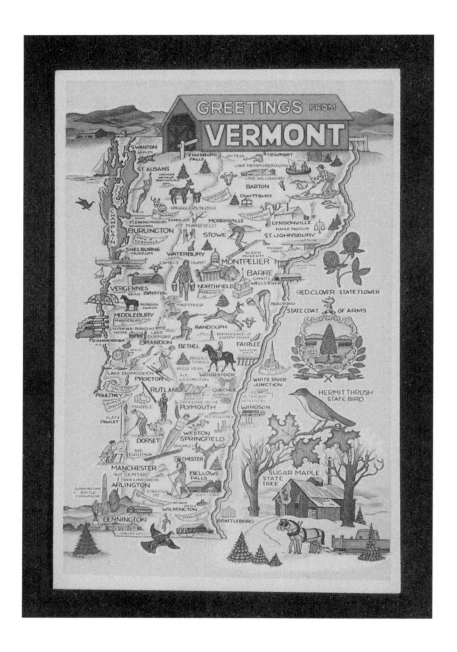

Vermont is home to mountains and hills covered with 80% forest that is the perfect example of New England scenery. If the outdoors isn't your thing, then you can enjoy the slower pace of small Colonial-era towns.

Vermont is home to the Green Mountains that has over 220 peaks of 2,000 feet or higher. If hiking is your thing, then head to the Green Mountain National Forest for the famous Appalachian Trail or the Long Trail. In the winter months, you can visit 20 alpine ski resorts, 7,300 acres of snow terrain and 30 cross-country skiing sites.

If you'd rather hit the beach, then you should head to Lake Champlain Islands on the western border. Here you can enjoy over 200 miles of shoreline and a number of wildlife. You can even visit the Lake Champlain Maritime Museum to learn about the history of the lake and local archaeology.

When it comes to experiencing New England art, culture and history the best option is to visit Burlington, right on the shores of Lake Champlain. The city features a walkable downtown area with parks, eateries, and museums. If you visit in the spring and summer, you will be able to take part in a number of outdoor concerts and festivals.

SUGGESTED VERMONT RV TRIP

Vermont is a state you can enjoy year round. Take a short 111 mile trip through three cities that takes about two hours to drive and days to enjoy everything. Start your trip in the city of Montpelier. It is known as the smallest state capital in the United States. Downtown is full of bookstores, boutiques, and dining options. Spend a while enjoying the quaint and small town.

The second stop is the historic town of Woodstock. It takes about an hour to drive the 54 miles to this town located on the banks of the

Ottauquechee River on the Vermont Scenic Byway. The towns main fame is the gateway to the only national park in Vermont: the Marsh-Billings-Rockefeller National Historical Park.

The final stop in the trip is Manchester. It takes you about an hour and a half to travel the 57 miles to this destination. This is known as a resort town with a number of skiing and shopping options. However, the city also offers a number of history, culture and outdoor recreation options.

RV CAMPING AT VERMONT STATE PARKS

AMENITIES

- Typical Cost: $18-$22
- Water: No
- Electric: No
- Sewer: No
- In/Out Rules: 21 night maximum.

VERMONT STATE PARKS

- ❏ Elmore (45 primitive sites)
- ❏ Emerald Lake (67 primitive sites)
- ❏ Maidstone (34 primitive sites)
- ❏ Brighton (61 primitive sites)
- ❏ Big Deer (23 primitive sites)
- ❏ New Discovery (46 primitive sites)
- ❏ Ricker Pond (27 primitive sites)
- ❏ Stillwater (62 primitive sites)

- ❑ Quechee (45 primitive sites)
- ❑ Silver Lake (40 primitive sites)
- ❑ Branbury (17 primitive sites)
- ❑ Gifford Woods (22 primitive sites)
- ❑ Jamaica (41 primitive sites)
- ❑ Mt. Ascutney (39 primitive sites)
- ❑ Coolidge (26 primitive sites)
- ❑ Fort Dummer (50 primitive sites)
- ❑ Molly Stark (23 primitive sites)
- ❑ Woodford (103 primitive sites)
- ❑ Townshend (30 primitive sites)
- ❑ Wilgus (17 primitive sites)
- ❑ Half Moon Pond (52 primitive sites)
- ❑ Branbury (17 primitive sites)
- ❑ Bomoseen (56 primitive sites)
- ❑ Lake St. Catherine (50 primitive sites)
- ❑ Button Bay (60 primitive sites)
- ❑ Little River (81 primitive sites)
- ❑ Smugglers' Notch
- ❑ Lake Carmi (140 primitive sites)
- ❑ Burton Island (17 primitive sites)

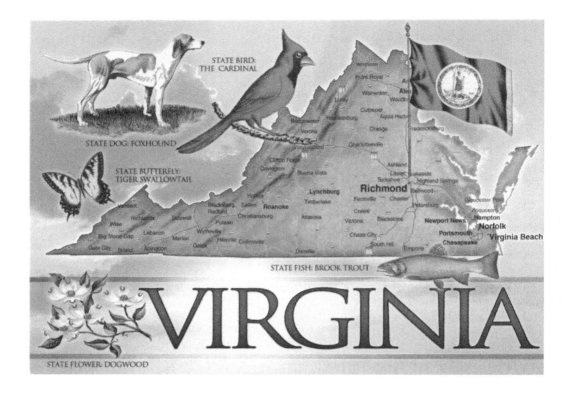

The best place to go to experience the history of the United States is Virginia. An English speaking colony was established in 1607 and since four of the first five presidents were born in the state and more Civil War battles were fought in Virginia than any other state. As a result, the state has more historic sights and living-history museums than most states. However, there are also plenty of beautiful outdoor attractions for those who want to spend time with nature.

Perhaps one beautiful place to visit the outdoors is Virginia Beach on the Atlantic coast near the North Carolina border. Here you'll see dense forest give way to golden sand. You can hike, kayak, sail or enjoy a three-mile boardwalk with eateries and live music. Nearby you can enjoy the

Back Bay National Wildlife Refuge with over 9,000 acres of coastline and a number of wildlife such as deer, raccoons, river otters, muskrats and a number of birds.

Another option to enjoy nature is the Assateague Island National Seashore that covers both Virginia and Maryland. It is a 37-mile long barrier island that serves as a wildlife sanctuary for shorebirds, waterfowl, dolphins, whales and wild ponies. There are a number of outdoor activities here including horseback, riding, hunting, camping, fishing, crabbing, hiking, kayaking, and seashell hunting.

If you want to spend more time on land, then consider the Shenandoah National Park in the Blue Ridge Mountains. At this park, there are over 60 peaks, 100 varieties of trees and plenty of animal species. This park has over 500 miles of hiking trails, or you can drive the beautiful Skyline Drive.

When it comes to history-filled cities, you should head to Arlington just across the water from Washington D.C. Here you'll find a number of landmarks that rival those in the capital. You can tour the Pentagon or walk through Arlington National Cemetery. Arlington is also home to urban villages with boutiques and theaters, so you are sure to find something to do no matter what your interests are.

Richmond is the capital of Virginia and another city full of history. You can take the Liberty Trail, which is a self-guided walking path that takes you past fifteen historic sites. There is also a number of wine trails here that take you through the almost 300 wineries.

No trip to Virginia for a history buff is complete without visiting Colonial National Historical Park. This park includes two important historical sites: Jamestown Settlement and Yorktown Battlefield. Jamestown was the site of English landfall in 1607, and the 1781 Battle of Yorktown was a key victory for the Colonial Army during the Revolution.

SUGGESTED VIRGINIA RV TRIP

An RV trip through Virginia is sure to give you a diverse range of things to see and do, no matter what your interest is. This suggested trip will take you through a range of five cities in about five hours while traveling 265 miles. Start your trip out in the beautiful Shenandoah Valley at the town of Staunton.

Here you'll find a number of cultural and historical attractions. A must see is the Frontier Cultural Museum that shows the story of the early days of America. In the historic downtown area, you'll also be able to visit the birthplace of President Woodrow Wilson. You may also want to check out the American Shakespeare Center and enjoy a play.

The second stop on your trip is the urban center of Richmond. It takes you about two hours to get about 108 miles down the road. The Richmond area was settled in the early 1600s and served as a turning point in both the Revolutionary and Civil Wars. A must see is the American Civil War Museum. Other places to see is the Virginia Museum of Fine Arts, the State Capitol, and the Lewis Ginter Botanical Gardens.

Next, take a short 52-minute drive about 51 miles down the road to the town of Williamsburg. Here you must visit Colonial Williamsburg, the largest and most authentic outdoor museum dedicated to colonial life. Also in the area, you want to visit the American Revolution Museum, the Yorktown Battlefield, and the Jamestown Settlement. For families, you can visit Busch Gardens or Water Country.

Your next stop is about 60 miles down the road in Virginia Beach, a drive of about an hour. This town is located along the Atlantic Ocean and has a lot of beautiful beaches to explore. It is also home to an enormous 59 block boardwalk. Be sure to stop by the First Landing State Park where the Jamestown settlers first landed in 1607.

End your trip with a short hour-long drive about 47 miles down the road to Cape Charles. This town is located on the Chesapeake Bay and features a number of examples of late-Victorian architecture.

Be sure to take a stroll along the historic Town Harbor waterfront and stop by the Cape Charles Museum. At the mouth of the bay, you will want to visit Cape Charles and Cape Henry Lights. Get outdoors at the Eastern Shore National Wildlife Refuge.

RV CAMPING AT VIRGINIA STATE PARKS

AMENITIES

- Typical Cost: $15-$24
- Water: Yes
- Electric: Yes
- Sewer: Rarely (2 out of 22 parks)
- In/Out Rules: 14 days out of 30.

- ❏ Hungry Mother (42 water & electric, 30 full hookups)
- ❏ Grayson Highlands (41 water & electric, 32 primitive sites)
- ❏ Claytor Lake (40 water & electric, 70 primitive sites)
- ❏ Fairy Stone (50 water & electric)
- ❏ Smith Mountain Lake (24 water & electric)
- ❏ Douthat (68 water & electric, 19 primitive sites)
- ❏ Staunton River (34 water & electric)
- ❏ Occoneechee (39 water & electric, 9 primitive sites)
- ❏ Twin Lakes (33 water & electric)
- ❏ Holliday Lake (36 water & electric)
- ❏ James River (40 water & electric)
- ❏ Bear Creek Lake (37 water & electric)
- ❏ Pocahontas (114 water & electric)
- ❏ Lake Anna (23 water & electric, 23 primitive sites)
- ❏ Shenandoah River (32 water & electric, 10 primitive sites)
- ❏ Westmoreland (42 water & electric, 74 primitive sites)
- ❏ Belle Isle (28 water & electric)
- ❏ Chippokes Plantation (50 water & electric)
- ❏ Kiptopeke (54 water & electric, 32 full hookups, 5 primitive sites)
- ❏ First Landing (107 water & electric, 81 primitive sites)
- ❏ Breaks Park (115 water & electric, 9 primitive sites)
- ❏ Natural Tunnel (34 water & electric)

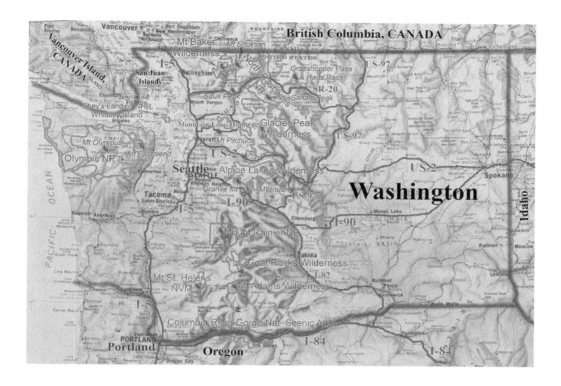

In the Pacific Northwest, Washington offers a combination of rugged mountains, beautiful beaches, urban centers and quaint villages. This means plenty of activities and things to see for all travelers.

Washington offers a number of natural playgrounds ranging from rainforests to coastlines to mountains. One of the best places to experience this is Olympic National Park, a part of the huge Olympic Peninsula. This massive park is just shy of a million acres and features three unique ecosystems. The park includes dozens of beaches, while Hurricane Ridge is home to a wildflower peninsula and then the west side of the park is home to the Hoh Rain Forest.

Another incredible outdoor experience is found at Mount Rainier National Park. The feature is the 14,410 foot Mount Rainier that is an active volcano. Here you can take in a number of hiking trails with a variety of breathtaking vistas.

If you want to spend time on the beach, then head to Puget Sound. Here you'll find over 170 islands with plenty of swimming, surfing, kayaking and cycling options. Over 80 of the islands are protected by the San Juan Islands Wildlife Refuge for seals, sea lions, seabirds and orca whales.

For the urban trip, you want to stop by Seattle. Here you can visit the 605 foot tall Space Needle built for the 1962 World's Fair. Next door is the interactive Experience Music Museum of Pop Culture that focuses on preserving science fiction, music, and art. If you want to get away from the big city and go someplace a little slower, Olympia is your destination. Here you'll find the State Capitol Building, Old Capitol Building, and several historic homes.

SUGGESTED WASHINGTON RV TRIP

While many think of Washington as a place to go to enjoy the great outdoors, there is actually a wonderful winery tour to enjoy on an RV trip of the state. It takes you 277 miles on a four and a half hour drive through six cities.

Start your trip out in the famous city of Seattle. While seeing popular sites such as the Space Needle, there is also a strong wine scene in town to enjoy. Just a few to consider include: Charles Smith Wines Jet City, Eight Bells Winery, Robert Ramsay Cellars and Domanico Cellars.

SUGGESTED RV PARK IN SEATTLE

If you need a little extra time to enjoy all Seattle has to offer then consider staying a few nights at Lake Pleasant RV Park in the nearby town of Bothell. This is a 198 site RV park that costs $44 and is open all year. It is pet-friendly and offers the following amenities:

★ Internet
★ Restrooms and Showers
★ Laundry
★ RV Supplies
★ Metered LP Gas
★ Ice
★ Self-Service RV Wash
★ Recreation Hall
★ Playground
★ Outdoor Games
★ Nature Trails
★ Putting Green

The second stop on your trip is the small town of Ellensburg. It is 107 miles down the road and takes about two hours to get there. Some top wineries to visit while here include: Elevage Wine Co., Thrall and Dodge Winery, Swiftwater Cellars, Springboard Winery and Gard Vintners. You'll also want to stop by The Ellensburg Distillery to see how they make lavender-infused Amethyst Gin.

Your next stop is a short 36-mile trip about 41 minutes down the road. The Yakima Valley has the biggest concentration of wineries in the state. The sunny region here is similar to the wine growing regions in France.

The fourth stop is the town of Prosser. A short 49-minute drive to cover about 49 miles. Here you can enjoy a number of festivals such as the Great Prosser Balloon Rally and Harvest Festival if you are traveling in September.

SUGGESTED RV PARK IN PROSSER

If you need more time at festivals or wineries in the area, then you should consider staying at Wine Country RV Park. This 125 space RV Park is open all year at the cost of $33 to $61. It is pet-friendly with the following amenities:

- ★ Internet
- ★ Restrooms and Showers
- ★ Laundry
- ★ RV Supplies
- ★ Metered LP Gas
- ★ Firewood
- ★ Ice
- ★ Groceries
- ★ Onsite RV Service
- ★ Cable
- ★ Guest Services
- ★ Heated Pool
- ★ Hot Tub
- ★ Horseshoes

- ★ Recreation Hall
- ★ Playground
- ★ Pavilion
- ★ Nature Trails
- ★ Putting Green

The next stop is actually a Tri-Cities area that includes Pasco, Richland, and Kennewick. It takes you about 30 minutes and 30 miles to get there. This area features a couple of hundred wineries within a 50-mile radius. A must visit winery is Chateau Ste. Michelle.

SUGGESTED RV PARK AROUND TRI-CITIES

If you need extra time explore all these wineries consider staying at the Horn Rapids RV Resort in Richland. This 225 space RV Park is open all year at the cost of $42. It is pet-friendly with an enclosed dog run and the following human amenities:

- ★ Restrooms and Showers
- ★ Laundry
- ★ RV Supplies
- ★ Metered LP Gas
- ★ Ice
- ★ Snack Bar
- ★ Groceries
- ★ Onsite RV Service
- ★ Cable
- ★ Self-Service RV Wash
- ★ Heated Pool

- ★ Hot Tub
- ★ Horseshoes
- ★ Recreation Hall
- ★ Playground
- ★ Outdoor Games
- ★ Pavilion
- ★ Shuffleboard

Travel about 55 miles down the road with about an hour drive to reach your final destination of Walla Walla. Located in the foothills of the Blue Mountains, this town has plenty of wineries and outdoor activities. There are over 100 wineries in the area with tasting rooms. A must visit is the Northstar Winery.

RV CAMPING AT WASHINGTON STATE PARKS

AMENITIES

- Typical Cost: $12-$45
- Water: Usually (57 out of 67 parks)
- Electric: Usually (57 out of 67 parks)
- Sewer: Sometimes (31 out of 67 parks)
- In/Out Rules: 10 days maximum April through September, 20 days otherwise.

WASHINGTON STATE PARKS

- ❏ Alta Lake (34 water & electric)
- ❏ Battle Ground Lake (25 water & electric, 25 primitive sites)
- ❏ Bay View (30 water & electric)

- ❑ Beacon Rock (5 full hookups, 26 primitive sites)
- ❑ Belfair (19 full hookups, 37 additional sites)
- ❑ Birch Bay (20 water & electric, 149 primitive sites)
- ❑ Blake Island (44 primitive sites)
- ❑ Bogachiel (6 water & electric, 26 primitive sites)
- ❑ Bridgeport (20 water & electric)
- ❑ Brooks Memorial (23 full hookups)
- ❑ Camano Island (88 primitive sites)
- ❑ Cape Disappointment (60 full hookups, 18 water & electric, 137 primitive sites)
- ❑ Columbia Hills (8 water & electric)
- ❑ Conconully (20 water & electric)
- ❑ Curlew Lake (18 full hookups, 7 water & electric)
- ❑ Daroga (28 water & electric)
- ❑ Dash Point (27 full hookups, 114 primitive sites)
- ❑ Deception Pass (143 water & electric)
- ❑ Dosewallips (45 full hookups, 10 water & electric, 70 primitive sites)
- ❑ Fields Spring (20 primitive sites)
- ❑ Fort Casey (14 water & electric, 21 primitive sites)
- ❑ Fort Ebey (11 water & electric, 39 primitive sites)
- ❑ Fort Flagler (55 full hookups, 59 primitive sites)
- ❑ Fort Townsend (40 primitive sites)
- ❑ Fort Worden State Park and Conference Center (50 full hookups, 30 water & electric)
- ❑ Ginkgo / Wanapum (50 full hookups)
- ❑ Grayland Beach (58 full hookups, 38 water & electric)
- ❑ Ike Kinswa (41 full hookups, 31 water & electric, 31 primitive sites)

- ❏ Illahee (2 full hookups, 23 primitive sites)
- ❏ Jarrell Cove (22 primitive sites)
- ❏ Kanaskat-Palmer (19 electric)
- ❏ Kitsap Memorial (18 water & electric, 21 primitive sites)
- ❏ Lake Chelan (17 full hookups, 18 water & electric)
- ❏ Lake Easton (45 full hookups)
- ❏ Lake Sylvia (4 water & electric)
- ❏ Lake Wenatchee (42 water & electric)
- ❏ Larrabee (26 full hookups)
- ❏ Lewis & Clark (9 full hookups)
- ❏ Lewis & Clark Trail (24 primitive sites)
- ❏ Lincoln Rock (32 full hookups, 35 water & electric)
- ❏ Manchester (15 water & electric)
- ❏ Maryhill (50 full hookups)
- ❏ Millersylvania (48 water & electric)
- ❏ Moran (151 primitive sites)
- ❏ Mount Spokane (8 primitive sites)
- ❏ Ocean City (29 full hookups, 149 primitive sites)
- ❏ Pacific Beach (42 electric, 18 primitive sites)
- ❏ Paradise Point (18 water & electric)
- ❏ Pearrygin Lake (50 full hookups, 27 water & electric, 76 primitive sites)
- ❏ Potholes (60 full hookups)
- ❏ Potlatch (35 water & electric)
- ❏ Rainbow Falls (8 water & electric, 39 primitive sites)
- ❏ Rasar (20 water & electric, 18 primitive sites)
- ❏ Riverside (16 water & electric, 16 primitive sites)
- ❏ Saltwater (47 primitive sites)
- ❏ Scenic Beach (18 sites)

- ❏ Schafer (9 water & electric)
- ❏ Seaquest (33 sites, some with full hookups)
- ❏ Sequim Bay (15 full hookups)
- ❏ South Whidbey (8 water & electric)
- ❏ Steamboat Rock (136 full hookups)
- ❏ Sun Lakes (39 full hookups)
- ❏ Twanoh (22 full hookups)
- ❏ Twenty-Five Mile Creek (13 full hookups, 8 water & electric)
- ❏ Twin Harbors (42 full hookups)
- ❏ Wenatchee Confluence (51 full hookups)
- ❏ Yakima Sportsman (37 full hookups)

West Virginia is known as an outdoor adventure capital with over 226,500 acres of state parks and recreation spots. You'll find everything from rivers to mountain, caverns to forests. No matter what outdoor activities you enjoy, you're sure to find a destination to enjoy in West Virginia. However, the state is also home to a number of historic towns and villages.

Visit the New River Gorge National River to see one of the oldest waterways in the United States. Nearly 70,000 acres of land along the river offers plenty of activities both on and off the water. Another option is the Blackwater Falls State Park, home to several spectacular waterfalls. If you want to explore underground, then visit Lost World Caverns and Seneca Caverns.

For the urban traveler, you want to head to the state capital of Charleston. Here you can visit a number of historic buildings along Capitol Street or visit the exhibits at West Virginia State Museum. Charleston is also home to several festivals and events year round.

SUGGESTED WEST VIRGINIA RV TRIP

West Virginia is an outdoor lover's paradise. Take a 105-mile trip through three main cities to see the best that this state has to offer. Drive time is about two and a half hours, but there is plenty to see and do for days.

Start your trip out in the capital city of Charleston. This town is located between the Elk and Kanawha Rivers, making water activities a major draw. For indoor activities, you need to stop by the West Virginia State Museum to learn about the area dating back to 1788. You can also find a number of festivals year-round that focuses on arts and culture.

The middle point in this trip is the town of Fayetteville. It is about an hour drive down the road or about 51 miles. This town has a population of less than 3,000, but there is plenty to see and do. Whitewater rafting is big here.

End your trip by driving about 54 miles down the road to the town of Lewisburg. It will take you about an hour to travel this distance. The focus here is on the arts with plenty of theater, music and museum options. Be sure to stop by the Greenbrier Historical Society and North House Museum.

RV CAMPING AT WEST VIRGINIA STATE PARKS

AMENITIES

- Typical Cost: $12-$32
- Water: Sometimes (12 out of 29 parks)
- Electric: Yes
- Sewer: Rarely (6 out of 29 parks)
- Laundry: Sometimes (At resort parks)
- In/Out Rules: 14 days maximum with exceptions granted in Fall, Winter, and Spring.

WEST VIRGINIA STATE PARKS

- ❏ Audra (6 electric, 61 primitive sites)
- ❏ Babcock (52 sites, some with electric)
- ❏ Beech Fork (49 full hookups, 49 electric)
- ❏ Blackwater Falls (30 electric, 35 primitive sites)
- ❏ Bluestone (7 water & electric, 15 electric, 10 primitive sites)
- ❏ Camp Creek (3 full hookups, 7 water & electric, 16 electric)
- ❏ Canaan Valley Resort (57 full hookups)
- ❏ Cedar Creek (65 water & electric)
- ❏ Chief Logan (14 full hookups, 12 water & electric)
- ❏ Holly River (88 electric)
- ❏ Little Beaver (30 water & electric, 16 water)
- ❏ Moncove Lake (25 electric, 23 primitive sites)

- ❏ North Bend (28 water & electric, 26 electric, 24 primitive sites)
- ❏ Pipestem (21 full hookups, 19 electric, 32 primitive sites)
- ❏ Stonewall Jackson (multiple hookup sites)
- ❏ Tomlinson Run (39 electric, 15 primitive sites)
- ❏ Twin Falls (25 electric, 25 primitive sites)
- ❏ Tygart Lake (14 electric, 26 primitive sites)
- ❏ Watoga (50 electric, 38 primitive sites)

WEST VIRGINIA STATE FORESTS

- ❏ Cabwaylingo (6 water & electric, 17 primitive sites)
- ❏ Coopers Rock (25 electric)
- ❏ Greenbrier (16 electric)
- ❏ Kanawha (46 water & electric)
- ❏ Kumbrabow (13 sites)
- ❏ Seneca (10 primitive sites)

WEST VIRGINIA WILDLIFE MANAGEMENT AREAS

- ❏ Berwind Lake (8 sites)
- ❏ Bluestone (hundreds of sites)
- ❏ Panther (6 electric)
- ❏ Plum Orchard Lake (38 sites)

WISCONSIN

Wisconsin is a state of a lot more than cheese. Nearly 10,000 years ago this land was carved out by glaciers that are now home to over 15,000 lakes and rivers surrounded by prairies and mountains. The best place to visit the great outdoors in Wisconsin is the Apostle Islands National Lakeshore. This area is made up of 21 islands in Lake Superior, which features more beaches and lighthouses than any other national park.

For the urban traveler, you want to head to Milwaukee along the eastern shore of Lake Michigan. Here you can tour a number of breweries or visit the Harley-Davidson Museum. For a small town visit head to Madison, home to the State Historical Museum and Veterans Museum.

SUGGESTED WISCONSIN RV TRIP

Wisconsin is a state filled with history and outdoor adventure. Experience both when you travel through five cities on a short 90-mile trip that takes about two hours and offers plenty to see and do.

Start your trip in the biggest town on the RV trip, Sturgeon Bay. It is a town full of wineries, breweries, farmers markets and museums. Two must-sees are the Door County Maritime Museum and the Door County Historical Museum. For the family, be sure to stop by The Farm to visit with baby goats and other farm animals.

Your second stop is a short 25-minute drive of about 17 miles to Egg Harbor. This small town is home to 200 people. Yet the area is home to beautiful scenery, golf courses, art galleries and a number of fun celebrations throughout the year.

Next, take another brief 21-minute drive about 12 miles down the road to the small town of Ephraim. This town was originally founded in 1853 as a Norwegian Moravian religious community and today is a beautiful waterfront town with a historic district. Enjoy a performance at Northern Sky Theater, play golf at Peninsula State Park Golf Course or related at The Spa at Sacred Grounds.

Drive another 16 miles down the road in about 27 minutes to reach the town of Northport. This is a very quiet and calm town popular with birding enthusiasts and photographers. Take a ferry over to Washington Island and drive their highways for a breathtaking view of the area. Be sure to stop by the Maritime Museum and the Art and Nature Center.

End your trip by heading back south about 21 miles for about 32 minutes to reach the town of Bailey's Harbor. Be sure to visit the historic Cana Island Lighthouse. If you want you can take a guided fishing tour, visit the lake in a glass-bottom kayak or take a zip line. Once you are done, you can drive about 22 miles back to Sturgeon Bay to complete the RV trip.

RV CAMPING AT WISCONSIN STATE PARKS

AMENITIES

- Typical Cost: $14-$22
- Water: No
- Electric: Usually
- Sewer: No
- In/Out Rules: 14 days in a 21 day period.

WISCONSIN STATE PARKS

- ❏ Amnicon Falls (36 sites)
- ❏ Big Bay (38 sites, 15 electric)
- ❏ Big Foot Beach (29 sites, 32 electric)
- ❏ Blue Mound (27 sites, 18 electric)
- ❏ Brunet Island (34 sites, 15 electric)

- ❑ Buckhorn (59 sites, 10 electric)
- ❑ Copper Falls (21 sites, 24 electric)
- ❑ Council Grounds (33 sites, 19 electric)
- ❑ Devil's Lake (178 sites, 121 electric)
- ❑ Governor Dodge (75 sites, 57 electric)
- ❑ Governor Thompson (84 sites, 16 electric)
- ❑ Harrington Beach (26 sites, 29 electric)
- ❑ Hartman Creek (54 sites, 24 electric)
- ❑ High Cliff (77 sites, 30 electric)
- ❑ Interstate (34 sites, 23 electric)
- ❑ Kohler-Andrae (54 sites, 68 electric)
- ❑ Lake Wissota (57 sites, 59 electric)
- ❑ Merrick (32 sites, 22 electric)
- ❑ Mill Bluff (15 sites, 6 electric)
- ❑ Mirror Lake (76 sites, 34 electric)
- ❑ Nelson Dewey (11 sites, 18 electric)
- ❑ New Glarus Woods (17 sites)
- ❑ Pattison (38 sites, 17 electric)
- ❑ Peninsula (299 sites, 157 electric)
- ❑ Perrot (43 sites, 36 electric)
- ❑ Potawatomi (56 sites, 39 electric)
- ❑ Roche-A-Cri (30 sites, 5 electric)
- ❑ Rocky Arbor (61 sites, 17 electric)
- ❑ Wildcat Mountain (15 sites)
- ❑ Willow River (95 sites, 55 electric)
- ❑ Wyalusing (53 sites, 26 electric)
- ❑ Yellowstone (50 sites, 24 electric)

WYOMING

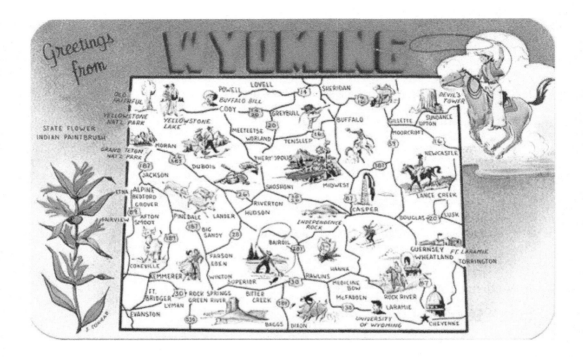

Wyoming is a place of rugged beauty where the Wild West still lives. Some of the oldest national parks in the United States can be found in Wyoming. The state is home to the lowest population of any state, making it ideal for the outdoor adventurer.

The northwest corner of the state is home to Yellowstone National Park, the first national park in the United States. Here you have nearly two million acres to explore with a variety of ecosystems and wildlife. It is also home to the largest number of geysers and thermal features anywhere. To the south, you can find Grand Teton National Park with 12 peaks over 12,000 feet. This is the perfect stop for hikers and climbers.

Visit any of Wyoming's cities to step back in time to the old west while still visiting a thriving urban center. Cheyenne is home to the Frontier Days Old West Museum, and in July you can visit the Cheyenne Frontier Days Rodeo, a ten-day event. The most packed historical city is Cody. This city consists of five museums including Draper Natural History Museum, Cody Firearms Museum, Whitney Western Art Museum, Buffalo Bill Museum and Plains Indian Museum.

SUGGESTED WYOMING RV TRIP

Wyoming is the least populated state but offers plenty of scenic wonders to enjoy. Enjoy all the natural wonders of Wyoming by traveling 490 miles between Cheyenne and Yellowstone. It will take you about eight hours to drive, but you'll have plenty to do for days.

Start your trip out in the state capital that is an example of the true West. If you visit in July, you'll be able to enjoy the Frontier Days Festival with a rodeo, concerts, food, and exhibits. While in Cheyenne, be sure to visit the Cheyenne Botanic Gardens to see a solar-heated conservatory and a range of beautiful western plants.

The second stop is the town of Casper. It will take you about two and a half hours to cover the 178 miles. Casper was once a boomtown and today is rich in history. There are plenty of outdoor adventures to enjoy including historic trails, skiing, hiking, waterfalls, gardens and more.

Next head 215 miles down the road on the longest leg of the trip of about four and a half hours to the town of Cody. This town was founded by Buffalo Bill and still maintains its Wild West image. Be sure to visit the

Buffalo Bill Center of the West; it is a complex of five museums with plenty of exhibits to explore.

End your trip 97 miles down the road in about an hour to Yellowstone National Park. This is the nation's first park, and it is full of astounding things to see and do. The wildlife in the park includes grizzlies, bison, and wolves.

The water in this park features half of the world's geysers and the largest high-altitude lakes, rivers, and waterfalls in the country. At nearly 3,500 square miles you can spend days exploring this park.

RV CAMPING AT WYOMING STATE PARKS

AMENITIES

- Typical Cost: $6-$22
- Water: Rarely
- Electric: Rarely
- In/Out Rules: 14 days out of 30.

WYOMING STATE PARKS

- ❑ Boysen State Park (64 primitive sites)
- ❑ Buffalo Bill State Park (99 water & electric)
- ❑ Connor Battlefield Historic Sites (20 primitive sites)
- ❑ Curt Gowdy State Park (145 water & electric)
- ❑ Glendo State Park (435 primitive sites)
- ❑ Guernsey State Park (240 primitive sites)
- ❑ Hawk Springs State Recreation Area (24 primitive sites)

- Keyhole State Park (283 water & electric)
- Medicine Lodge Archaeological Sites (25 primitive sites)
- Seminoe State Park (60 primitive sites)

CONCLUSION: TOP 5 LONG DISTANCE RV TRIPS

If you have extra time and want to take an extended RV road trip, then consider these five trips that take you across multiple states on an unforgettable journey.

ROUTE 66

This is the prime example of an old-fashioned US road trip. The total route covers 2,448 miles between Chicago and Los Angeles. As you travel you'll pass through cities, small towns and beautiful landscapes. Stops along the way will allow you to experience the evolution of modern American culture.

PACIFIC COAST HIGHWAY

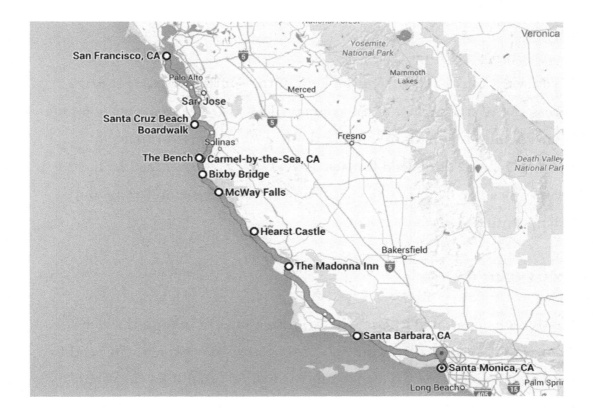

This is a wonderful and beautiful drive. You can even choose to pair this with a drive on Route 66 for an extended road trip. This coastal highway covers from Los Angeles to Olympia, Washington while passing through several well-known cities and towns. Along the way, you'll get to see some of the most beautiful scenery in the country ranging from sea to forest.

US-80

Taking a drive across the southern part of the country is a great way to experience history. Driving what was once US-80 will take you from San Diego to Savannah, Georgia. Along the way, you get to enjoy scenic wonders ranging from deserts, plains, and bayous. You'll also have a chance to see a range of cultures and sample the unique cuisine.

US-2

If you want to get away from the heat of the south, then take a drive across the northern part of the country. This trip covers over 2,500 miles from Washington to Maine. Along the way, you'll pass prairies, mountains, and hardwood forests. Traveling US-2 is a must for nature lovers since you'll get to enjoy stunning vistas more than towns and urban centers.

ATLANTIC COAST

Lastly, consider a drive along the Atlantic Coast to take in the rich American history and stunning coastal beauty. However, you'll need to plan ahead since this trip doesn't follow a single road like the others. Rather you'll want to avoid I-95 and stick mostly to scenic byways. When you do this, you'll be able to visit a number of historic colonial sites and quaint New England towns. This 2,400-mile coastal adventure will take you past a number of stunning landmarks including quite a few lighthouses from Maine to Florida.

LAST WORDS

Hopefully, in this book, I was able to give you a good general overview of RV traveling throughout our great country.

I wanted to thank you for buying my book; I am neither a professional writer nor an author, but rather a person who always has the passion for travel. In this book, I wanted to share my knowledge with you, as I know there are many people who share the same passion and drive as I do. So, this book is entirely dedicated to YOU, my readers.

Despite my best effort to make this book error free, if you happen to find any mistakes, I want to ask for your forgiveness ahead of time.

Just remember, my writing skills may not be best, but the knowledge I share here is pure and honest.

If you thought I added some value and shared some valuable information that you can use, please take a minute and post a review on wherever you bought this book from. This will mean the world to me. Thank you so much!!

Lastly, I wanted to thank my wife Rebecca for all her tireless help and support throughout this book, without her, this book would not have been possible.

Thank you once again and be safe.

Highland Hammock State Park
5931 Hammock Rd
Sebring, Florida 33872

863 · 386 · 6094

Tanglewood RV Resort
3000 Tanglewood Pkwy
Sebring
863 - 402 - 1500

Blue Springs State Park   sites
2100 West French Ave   54   002, 3, 4
Orange City, FL   33   or 27
386 775 - 3663   16   (33)
Res. 800 326. 3521   21
Reserve. America   Florida State Park   29
800 · 326 - 3521   19
                      FSP / reserve America. Com
www. Reserve America . Com
* Sm Text feature.

RV. Net   for question

Made in the USA
Columbia, SC
16 April 2019